Great Breeders and Their Methods
Leslie Combs II and Spendthrift Farm

by Mary Marshall

The Russell Meerdink Company, Ltd.
Neenah, Wisconsin 54956 U.S.A.

Copyright © 2008 by The Russell Meerdink Company, Ltd.

All Rights Reserved. No part of this book may be reproduced or transmitted in any form or by any means, electronic or mechanical, including photocopying, recording or by any information storage or retrieval system, without permission in writing from the publisher. Requests for permission should be addressed to The Russell Meerdink Company, Ltd., 1555 South Park Avenue, Neenah, WI 54956 USA.

Cover design & layout by Bosetti Production Art & Design

Library of Congress Cataloging-in-Publication Data

Marshall, Mary, 1963-
 Great breeders and their methods : Leslie Combs and Spendthrift Farm / by Mary Marshall.
   p. cm.
 ISBN 978-0-929346-82-3 (hardcover)
 1. Combs, Leslie. 2. Horse breeders--Kentucky--Lexington--Biography. 3. Race horses--Breeding--Kentucky--Lexington. 4. Thoroughbred horse--Breeding--Kentucky--Lexington. 5. Spendthrift Farm--History. I. Title.
 SF336.C66M37 2007
 636.1'322092--dc22
 [B]
                                        2007046220

Published by

The Russell Meerdink Company, Ltd.
1555 South Park Avenue, Neenah, Wisconsin 54956
USA
(920) 725-0955
www.horseinfo.com

Printed in the United States of America

TABLE OF CONTENTS

	Introduction	.5
Chapter 1	The Foundation	.9
Chapter 2	Spendthrift the Namesake	.21
Chapter 3	The Master Salesman	.27
Chapter 4	The Great Syndicator	.37
Chapter 5	Swaps for Nashua	.49
Chapter 6	Myrtlewood	.65
Chapter 7	Idun	.73
Chapter 8	Gallant Man	.79
Chapter 9	Raise a Native and His Line	.85
Chapter 10	Majestic Prince	.99
Chapter 11	Mr. Prospector	.105
Chapter 12	Landaluce	.113
Chapter 13	Breeding a Good Horse	.119
Chapter 14	Combs' Thoroughbred Club of America Address	.137
Chapter 15	Dorothy Enslow Combs	.143
Chapter 16	Revival and Reorganization	.147
Chapter 17	The Final Years	.155
	Spendthrift Stallions	.163
	Stakes Winners	.173

INTRODUCTION

It was a common pathway that led to my uncommon interest in Spendthrift Farm. When I was four years old in 1967, my parents and I were among the hundreds of thousands of visitors that wandered through the gates of Spendthrift only to be left in awe by the sheer beauty of the horses, the farm, and the vastness of its proportions.

We had just moved to Kentucky from Wisconsin, and even at that tender age I was absolutely horse crazy and couldn't get enough exposure. My father was a wildlife professor and my mother, a Stanford-educated housewife. They were extremely well-rounded people, who had seen a great deal of the world, but were primarily non-horsey. I feel certain that they were slightly befuddled at their daughter's overwhelming squeals of delight at the antics of these galloping, snorting creatures as they sped around the field. Regardless, they fostered my interest and lifetime love of animals of all kinds.

We arrived at Spendthrift on a weekday afternoon when there were very few visitors on the grounds. My memories of the day are as vivid as if it were yesterday. I bounded out of the car, and took off full tilt toward the stallion barn with my parents scurrying after me. There was no containing my enthusiasm. Oh the sweet smell of horses, sweet feed, and straw! It was pure perfume! Without fear, I ran from stall to stall, petting Swaps on the nose, then Cornish Prince, sniffing noses with Nashua as he lowered his great head to determine my status, when a strong arm took me by the hand.

"Lil' girl that hoss'll take 'yer head off," crooned a voice as smooth as velvet. "C'mon over here. I got a good horse you can pet that likes little girls."

The strong arm and deep velvety voice belonged to none other than Spendthrift's famous groom Clem, whose smile was as broad as his aura was warm. I clenched Clem's big hand and eagerly wandered over to a stall where a handsome bay with a feathered star leaned out of the Dutch door and nuzzled the top of my head with his muzzle. Giggling, I reached up to touch his soft nose, and he groomed my topknot with his lip. "Now here's a hoss you can pet," said Clem convincingly. "This is Gallant Man. He's a kind hoss, and wouldn't dream of biting anybody."

My parents, by this time, were beginning to feel a bit lightheaded as they attempted to keep up with me and my antics as I galloped through the Spendthrift stallion barn. Mom, relieved that I hadn't bolted into a stall, gave a great sigh and took a seat while Dad, oblivious to the possible danger, took pictures. Joyously, I reached for Gallant Man's halter, and celebrated the moment on tiptoes with a monumental grin. At that precise moment, I was in horse heaven.

The visit to Spendthrift fostered an interest in the farm's stallions and their careers. Throughout childhood, I studied their bloodlines, scanned the newspapers and magazines for articles on the Spendthrift horses, and devoured Thoroughbred books until there were no more to check out in the library. My interest in horses branched out into other breeds along with Thoroughbreds, but I never lost track of Gallant Man.

In 1988, I worked as the associate editor for the Horseman's Journal magazine, which was based in Lexington at that time. The editor and I took our lunch hour, and decided to journey out to Spendthrift Farm to look at stallions.

Clem was gone by this time, but Gallant Man remained. Well into his thirties, the grand old man greeted me with a nicker, and shook his stall door with his teeth for effect. His eyes were deeply introspective and bright, and his bay face was scattered with gray hairs throughout. His ears had fuzzy "old horse" fur that protruded out to the sides, and his lower lip drooped somewhat. He was much smaller than I remembered, but just as large in character. The groom, obviously moved by my story, gladly opened the stall door and allowed me to reunite with my friend. Gallant Man nibbled at my jacket as I stroked his neck. He was obviously enjoying the attention, and stretched out in the stall so I could rub his girth.

Swaying back and forth with enjoyment, the old horse stretched out his neck and began to rub the groom with his lip.

"Whatever he gets these days he's more than earned," the groom emphasized. "This horse should have been a champion."

Gallant Man passed over the Rainbow Bridge shortly after my visit. He remains the champion of my heart. Gallant Man will always hold a unique place in my history with horses. The little horse who "should have been a champion" played an integral role, along with Swaps, Nashua, Raise a Native, Myrtlewood, Mr. Prospector, and others in the great success of Spendthrift Farm.

This book is dedicated to my parents, Molly and Ward Rudersdorf, who recognized that my interest in horses was the key to a lifetime of happiness and heapfuls of muck.

– Mary R. Marshall

CHAPTER ONE

THE FOUNDATION

Passing through the main gate of Spendthrift Farm, located on the old Iron Works Pike, the stately oak trees bow eloquently over the four-board paddocks where Thoroughbred mares and foals are still nourished by the nutritious grasses fed by the underground springs that flow beneath the fertile maury silt loam soils. The U-shaped stallion barn, built in the late 1950s when Nashua became the main attraction on the farm, still retains its old world charm as a shedrow barn with an open entrance and aisle. Colorful flowers and bushes bloom around the courtyard of the stallion barn, whose central focus is the statue of Nashua and his equally charismatic groom Clem Brooks, who entertained visitors for decades with the lore of Spendthrift's history and stallions. Listening closely, a visitor may still hear the rhythmic sound of Nashua's hoofbeats as they echo on the breeze, perhaps Gallant Man, Raise a Native, Swaps, Affirmed, or Seattle Slew. The energy radiates the glory of a bygone era, a time when racing was sport and the participants were sportsmen.

Leslie Combs vaulted himself to the forefront of the Kentucky Thoroughbred breeding industry with a vision and a shrewd business plan that became a reality. Spendthrift Farm was an original Combs creation whose roots began long before the Bluegrass began to grow behind the miles of black four-board fencing.

The Combs family came from a long line of distinguished Kentuckians, beginning with Benjamin Combs in 1755. Combs served under British Major General Edward Braddock, and fought in the French-Indian wars, including the defeat of Fort Duquesne. The tough old warrior also fought against the British in the American Revolution 20 years later, and eventually settled in Kentucky.

Benjamin's son was the colorful General Leslie Combs, who was captured by Indians during the War of 1812. The General was forced to run the gauntlet, and carried the scars of his ordeal for the remainder of his lifetime. General Combs eventually became Henry Clay's law partner, and built his home on the former site of Union Station located on Main Street in Lexington.

Leslie's great-grandfather was Daniel Swigert, considered one of the great horsemen of the 19th century. He had been the "head of the horse department" for Robert A. Alexander's famed Woodburn Stud near Versailles, Kentucky. Woodburn boasted among their stallion roster the great Lexington, listed as the most prolific sire in the United States during the 19th century.

After the death of Alexander in 1867, Woodburn was inherited by his brother, A.J. Alexander, who had little interest in horses.

Working under the younger Alexander, Swigert watched the farm's stock and reputation decline for two years before purchasing the 300-acre Stockwood Farm, which later became Elmendorf Farm in 1897 under the ownership of James "Ben Ali" Haggin. Swigert settled into his Paris Pike residence, and took up the business of breeding horses his own way. He became renowned as a breeder of outstanding Thoroughbreds, including three Kentucky Derby winners – Hindoo (1881), Apollo (1882), and Ben Ali (1886).

Swigert also owned Spendthrift Farm's namesake Spendthrift, whom he purchased from Alexander as a yearling and eventually sold to breeder James R. Keene. Spendthrift won the 1879 Belmont Stakes carrying the Keene silks. He also bred 1870 Belmont Stakes winner Kingfisher, the great race mare Firenze, and the unbeaten two-year-old Tremont. The leading stallions of the 1884-86 seasons, Glenelg and Virgil, stood at Swigert's Elmendorf Farm.

"Both my great-granddaddies raised horses," Combs confided in an interview with the Miami Herald in 1970. "General Leslie Combs was Henry Clay's law partner, and one of the first presidents of the Kentucky Association. His son, Leslie Jr., was Minister to Honduras and the first U.S. Ambassador to Peru. He (Leslie Jr.) raised me after my daddy, Daniel Swigert Combs, died."

The aristocratic Bluegrass legacy seemed to be firmly in place for the little boy born to Daniel and Florence Combs in rural Fayette County, Kentucky, on October 22, 1901. However, Leslie's early life was marred by tragedy. The humble beginnings of his younger days ignited a dogged determination and perseverance in a very observant and intelligent little boy who sought to achieve a milestone larger than any of the ancestors before him.

The set of circumstances that set the stage for Leslie's teenage years was triggered by the untimely death of his father. Daniel Combs lost his job as a cattle farm manager in Hickory Valley, Tennessee, in January, 1915. Depressed, in debt, and unable to find another job, Daniel fatally shot himself in the head at the age of 37. His wife, Florence, was left penniless, with $11,000 in debts and two children to raise, Leslie, 14, and his infant sister Elizabeth.

The options for Florence, who came from a modest family background, were limited due to the times in which she lived. She was a product of her generation, when motherhood and the duties of being a wife vastly overshadowed the concept of an advanced education and career for the average woman. Widowed and without a viable means of support, she sent young Leslie to live with relatives in her hometown of Lewisburg, West Virginia, where he attended the Greenbriar Military School. With his baby sister Elizabeth in tow, Florence temporarily moved into a boarding house in Frankfort, Kentucky. She eventually transferred to Washington, D.C. after Elizabeth died in 1917, and was employed as a clerk for the government. Florence died in 1964.

As a teenager, Leslie spent the summers with his grandparents at their opulent Belair Farm in southern Fayette County. His grandfather, Leslie Combs Jr., was a successful farmer and former U.S. Minister to Guatemala and Honduras, who married Swigert's daughter Mary.

The union produced two prominent Kentucky horsemen, Lucas Combs, who became a trustee of Keeneland, and Brownell Combs, the breeder of blue hen Myrtlewood.

Combs would later partner-up with his uncle into a successful breeding venture that yielded such amazing results as champion Myrtle Charm, and Gold Digger – the dam of Mr. Prospector.

"My uncle Brownell taught me all I know about horsemanship, and a few other things too," Leslie told The *Courier-Journal* in 1980. "I was about 18 and he called me one day, said 'Leslie, meet me at the Citizen's Bank, at 12:00. I want to see you.' I said 'Just fine, I'll be there.' So I got there about quarter past twelve, and he and Sidney Combs, my cousin, were coming out the door. And he said 'Oh hello Leslie. I thought maybe you weren't coming. You said you'd be here at 12. I had a couple of $5,000 bonds, and I was going to give you one and Sidney one. So as long as you weren't here, I just gave them both to Sydney.'"

The days of youth spent at Belair were formative ones for Leslie, as he wandered up and down the hallways of the large house admiring the vast heirlooms and ancestral portraits that adorned the walls. However the keen observations were far more than mere adolescent musings for the teenager, whose creative determination and shrewd eye for detail would create a breeding dynasty that far surpassed that of his ancestor Swigert.

After fulfilling the drudgery of a disciplined military education, Leslie was ready to kick up his heels. As a young adult his visits to the Bluegrass increased, and so did his frequency on the high society party circuit where the shy adolescent discovered that he had a flair for persuasive discourse and unrivaled charm.

Leslie became a regular on the society pages of the Lexington newspaper featuring all the whys and wherefores of the horsey set, much to his grandfather's disdain. Old Leslie Jr., who wanted his grandson to grow up to become more than an idle rich kid, decided it was time for a change.

Young Leslie wasn't especially thrilled with his grandfather's choice of a change in scenery. After passing the tests to enter Annapolis, Leslie changed his mind and opted for Centre College, located in the quiet rural town of Danville, Kentucky. It was hardly a fashionable atmosphere for the type of action that a young man craved. In spite of the limitations, Leslie immersed himself in the social life of Centre College in the fall of 1921, and was determined to make the best of it.

Not especially interested in academics, Leslie pledged the fraternity of Phi Delta Theta and joined the Praying Colonel's football team as a substitute end. He roomed with future Keeneland auctioneer George Swinebroad, and developed a lasting friendship. As a football player, Leslie was moderate at best, and sat on the bench for most of the season. He broke his leg and nose, and in spite of the injuries continued to enjoy the camaraderie of his teammates. During his time at Centre, Leslie shaved off a couple numbers from the end of his name. Originally Leslie IV, he became Leslie II due to teasing from schoolmates over his extended pedigree.

College did not seem to be a comfortable fit for the precocious young man who had other ideas about where he wanted to be in life. In December, 1922, Leslie dropped out of college and made his way back to Lexington.

Once again his grandfather Leslie Jr. intervened. One can only imagine the conversations between the older southern gentleman and the precocious young colt with modern ideas. In spite of the vast chasm between the generations, Leslie and his grandfather seemed to arrive at a satisfactory alternative. Adventure, with its family boundaries intact, would still provide the needed "life education" for the young man.

Leslie became a clerk for Uncle Herbert Schlubach's Schlubach-Sapper Co, a coffee planting and export business located in Guatemala, where he learned to speak Spanish and close a deal. While in South America he contracted malaria. After recovering from the disease, Leslie became dissatisfied once again, and after eight months left Schlubach-Sapper to become a laborer at American Rolling Mill Co., a sheet mill company, located in Ashland, Kentucky, near the West Virginia border.

The Spanish came in handy, as Leslie recalled, when he was boarding a stallion and some mares for an Argentine family who had let their bills fall in arrears. Conversing in Spanish in the office, the Argentines put together a plan to offer 10 inexpensive mares in one package and five quality mares in another and offer Leslie his choice in payment. One of the brothers, commenting that Combs was greedy, said he would go for the group of 10.

"So they said, 'You've been so nice, we want you to have your choice here.' I said, 'Well boys, you've been so nice to me in doing this,

I'll just take the five and leave the 10 for you all. Caramba! You should have heard them. The one jumped up and said, 'You sure fixed this up, now he has all five of the good ones."

During the time spent in Ashland, Leslie met his future wife, Dorothy Enslow of Huntington, West Virginia. Pretty and wealthy, Dorothy was one of the most eligible young women in Huntington. Her father, Frank Bliss Enslow, had been a prestigious attorney for the Chesapeake & Ohio Railway. He was also one of the founders of the Columbia Gas & Electric Co., which eventually became Columbia Gas System. Dorothy's mother Juliette also had extensive wealth and social ties as the daughter of Huntington's first mayor, Peter K. Buffington.

"Oh she (Dorothy Enslow) was pretty," Leslie recalled in 1967. "I was going with another little gal, and I met Dorothy at a party. I said to myself, 'You better change fillies right now.' She liked the same things I did, and her mother, Mrs. Frank Enslow, just loved any kind of horse. We'd go around to all the little fairs in the '30s, and she liked to go to Charles Town to the races with us."

Leslie married Dorothy in 1924, and moved into the family mansion with his widowed mother-in-law. He worked as a teller at the Huntington National Bank, and later became a partner in the insurance firm of Combs, Ritter, & Co. In the mid-1930s, his children, Juliette and Brownell, came along to complete the family portrait. Leslie became a polo player at the Greenbriar resort in Sulphur Springs, West Virginia, and became a member of the West Virginia Racing Commission. In spite of all the visible signs of success, Leslie still felt an itch for something bigger.

Tragedy interrupted the quest for success when Dorothy's mother was found beaten and strangled in her bedroom on October 17, 1936, in their home at 1307 Third Avenue on the prestigious "Millionaires Row." The murder, which is considered one of the most heinous crimes in the history of Huntington, took place between 10:30 p.m. on Friday night and 8:30 a.m. Saturday morning. After the initial investigation, the diamond rings and a studded diamond bracelet that Enslow wore to bed at night came up missing. The wristwatch was later located in a drawer in her bedroom.

Ten days after the murder, Charles Baldwin, Enslow's son from a previous marriage, was charged with the crime. After a heated and emotional trial, Baldwin was acquitted five months later on March 27. Leslie, luckily in Lexington on a business trip when the crime occurred, testified on behalf of the defense.

The murder has never been solved. However, on February 22, 1940, the *Huntington Herald-Dispatch* reported a new lead in the Enslow murder that made front page headlines. One of the diamond rings that had disappeared on the night of the murder, a large solitaire in a platinum setting with a black onyx mounting, was discovered by a city street department employee behind the Enslow Home in an alley catch basin within a short distance of the rear entry to the house. Although the discovery was startling indeed, there is no evidence that the police ever reopened the case.

Enslow left only one item to Leslie in her will, a collection of books written by the 19th Century French novelist Honore de Balzac. According to Balzac biographer V.S. Pritchett, the author was obsessed with social prestige "like one of the hard-faced, fortune-hunting characters who populate the 70 volumes of his Comedie Humaine." An interesting twist to a tragic tale.

Leslie and Dorothy decided to move to Lexington after the Enslow murder. That same year he received a monetary windfall of $600,000 following the death of his Grandmother Combs.

Leslie, a skilled horseman, wanted to continue the family tradition of raising Thoroughbreds in the Bluegrass. In September, 1937, Leslie bought 127 acres of the old Hugh Fontaine farm on the southern end of Ironworks Pike near Lexington.

Leslie knew that a farm needed well-bred mares to build a solid breeding foundation. Uncle Brownell gave him the esteemed mare Frizeur and her finest daughter, Myrtlewood. Nicknamed the "fleet bay mare of the '30s," Myrtlewood and her daughters became the anchor of the Spendthrift breeding program. Broodmares carrying a direct female line to Myrtlewood are still sought after by breeders today.

"In order to be able to sell," Combs said in a 1967 interview, "you've got to not only have stakes mares, but also the young daughters and granddaughters of great families."

The list of Spendthrift's success mounted over the coming years. Leslie rewrote the record books with one record after another: Spendthrift became the only commercial breeding operation whose farm-bred runners earned over $1 million in a single season, he became the only commercial breeder to sell two champions – Myrtle Charm and Idun, leading commercial breeder on the seasonal earnings list, the only commercial breeder to gross more than $1 million at one sale, consignor of the world's highest-priced auction yearling, holder of the highest Keeneland Summer Sales average on record, and the purchaser and syndicator of the first $1 million dollar-plus-stallion – Nashua.

By the early 1960s, Spendthrift Farm's burgeoning success was reflected in more than 5,000 acres of prime bluegrass farmland. Part of Leslie's holdings included 407 acres, purchased in 1962, of the Old Kenney Farm on Ironworks Pike and Russell Cave Road, which had formerly been the old ancestral home of Swigert's Stockwood Farm.

"Everybody said I was a damn fool to come in here," Leslie told *The Courier-Journal*. "They said, you got Walmac on that side of you. You've got the Whitney's over here, and the Wideners down here. How the hell you going to buy any land?"

At the height of Spendthrift's glory the farm was described in a 1964 *Thoroughbred Record* article as "being made up of at least a dozen units in addition to the original tract of land and main residence. Geographically varied in outline (some of the farms are not contiguous, although all lie within a five-mile radius bordering on such pikes as Russell Cave, Iron Works, Paris, Greenwich, and Harp and Innis, as well as Hume Road and Hughes Lane, in the northern part of Fayette County)...

"There are 10 complete farm units in all, including the main spread which provides quarters for the 30 stallions, 30 of Mr. Combs' own mares, some boarders, and all the sales yearlings. The other units are Spendthrift Farm numbers two through five, those being respectively the 'Widener Farm, Log Cabin Farm, the T.P. Hayes Farm, and the John J. Bryant Farm. Each farm has its own foreman who lives on the place, and its complement of grooms, so that each unit functions as a team, each horseman thoroughly familiar with each horse he handles.

"'You might say I took a page out of the Aly Kahn's book," Combs said. "You know he had several successful studs in Ireland and France, which were operated as separate but augmenting units."

When arriving to a conclusion regarding the name of the farm, it was not a difficult choice. Dorothy suggested, "Leslie your family has been in the Thoroughbred business for several generations here in Kentucky. Why don't we name the farm for its best horse?"

"Good idea," replied Leslie. "Guess that would have to be for one of the horses of my great-grandfather, Daniel Swigert – who was the foremost breeder of his day. Bred three Kentucky Derby winners in a space of six years before the turn of the century."

"Let me think..." Combs continued. "There was Spendthrift, whom he bought as a yearling. He was left at the post in the Belmont but came on and won it anyway. He was also the paternal great-grandsire of Man o' War."

Dorothy was listening intently. "Then there was Hindoo, whom he bred. He ran 35 times, won 30, 18 in a row including the Kentucky Derby. He sired Hanover and a lot of good..."

"Now Leslie," said his charming wife, "the farm's name won't be Hindoo!" So therefore the farm was christened Spendthrift.

Spendthrift was a Swigert champion with an interesting tale regarding the origin of his name. Mrs. Swigert returned to Kentucky after a shopping spree in New York, and Swigert, surprised by the amount she had spent, exclaimed that he was naming a colt for her and called the future champion Spendthrift. The following year, Mrs. Swigert jested that the full brother to Spendthrift should be named Miser. If the sarcastic spin on names had any influence on the individuals, it is ironic that Spendthrift proved to be the more successful racehorse and sire, while Miser inevitably faded into obscurity.

In the early days of Spendthrift's existence, Leslie got off to a promising start boarding horses and acting as manager for

Robert W. Mellwain's Walmac Farm on Paris Pike. Tradition is thick as molasses among the Bluegrass Thoroughbred breeders, and Leslie raised eyebrows as he outworked, outcharmed, and outmaneuvered the competition by utilizing other people's money to build Spendthrift from the ground up, and change the way that business was done, including the horse sales.

During World War II, economical restrictions on fuel and other supplies made it difficult for Thoroughbred breeders to transport their sale yearlings to Saratoga in New York for the annual sales venue in August. As a result, Keeneland founder and breeder Hal Price Headley headed up a group of Thoroughbred breeders, including Leslie, and formed the Breeders' Sales Company in 1944, which evolved into the world-famous Keeneland sales.

"Due to wartime restrictions, breeders found it impossible to ship their yearlings to Saratoga for the annual sales that had been the only market for many years," Combs recalled at the Thoroughbred Club of America's dinner honoring him in 1978. "Something had to be done about it, so a group of local horsemen organized the Breeders' Sales Company, and made an arrangement with Keeneland to use its facilities to hold a sale. The first sale was in a tent in the paddock and to the surprise of everyone, was an instant success. It grew by leaps and bounds, opening up a whole new untapped market in the Midwest."

An additional aspect of Leslie's life that better prepared him for a career in the Thoroughbred business was his influence on the conduct of racing when elected to West Virginia's first two racing commissions in the 1930s. He also gained his initial knowledge of racing protocol, rules, and regulations while serving as a patrol judge at the Old Raceland racetrack near Ashland, Kentucky.

In 1946, Leslie was selected as president of the National Association of State Racing Commissioners, after his initial appointment as a Kentucky State Racing Commissioner in 1943. He became a member of the elite Jockey Club in 1959, and was also a director of Keeneland Racecourse and Churchill Downs.

Spendthrift House, a 12-room Colonial mansion originally built in 1804, became the scene for many lavish parties, breakfasts, and dinner dances held during the Kentucky Derby and July summer yearling sales. The majority of Spendthrift's early clientele in the 1940s were the newly rich, ambitious businessmen, glamorous stars, and business moguls attracted by the lure of social prestige that came with owning horses. Leslie's reputation for good old-fashioned southern hospitality had spread nationwide, and he became known as "Cuzin' Leslie" to his friends and acquaintances. Cosmetics queen Elizabeth Arden Graham, publisher Jack Knight, Eugene Constantine, Mrs. Norman Woolworth, Marshall Field,

The Spendthrift residence. It is said that Leslie Combs would invite prospective buyers to the farm for dinner. As the guests dined, the mares and foals would graze along the fence line outside the dining room window. Leaving nothing to chance, he had sprinkled grain on the ground in just the right place to afford his guests the most pleasant view...and the guests all went home horse owners.

financier Louis Wolfson, former secretary of the treasury George Humphrey, Robert J. Kleberg (president of the famous King Ranch), John W. Hanes, Harry M. Warner, MGM mogul Louis B. Mayer, Fred Astaire, and Cadillac dealer Emil Denemark, the brother-in-law of gangster Al Capone, who sported a bulletproof vest and pistol in a shoulder holster – just in case – all became intertwined with the lore of Spendthrift Farm. Leslie could always mix and mingle with the most diverse crowd of people and make them feel at ease and comfortable, but you didn't dare walk away without at least a mint julep. So goes the story surrounding

Leslie and England's Princess Margaret, the sister to Queen Elizabeth II.

"When Princess Margaret was here, she came up to Spendthrift and had lunch with us," Combs recalled in the April 27, 1980, interview with the Louisville newspaper. "They told me you gotta bow and scrape and carry on and call her Your Royal Highness and all. So she came in and they introduced me to her and I said, 'Honey would you like a mint julep?' And she said 'I sure would.' And so I said, 'I'll fix you a good one in a gold cup here for you. It has about three jiggers of good ol' bourbon in it, you know, and she drank it down and said, 'Oh, could I hahve anothuh?' And she drank two, and then when she finished, she said, 'I think I'd like anothuh.' My God, she drank three of those. That's nine jiggers of bourbon. And you wouldn't know she'd ever drank 'em."

Leslie's favorite mode of transporting friends and clients to the races was partying en route on the famous Blue Goose, a Greyhound bus transformed into a custom coach with wood paneling and plush swivel chairs that was called "one of the most luxurious vehicles on the highway." The bus, which created an atmosphere of full-time revelry, was always stocked with "Old Spendthrift" bourbon, especially bottled for Leslie. Among the guests on the Blue Goose were then-California Governor Ronald Reagan, Michigan Representative Gerald Ford, and MaryLou Whitney, a close friend of Leslie, who also named the Whitney Blue Goose Stables after the bus. How did you get a ride on the famous bus? The best way to get invited to ride on the Blue Goose was to buy a horse from Combs, that is if you weren't a celebrity, relative, or close friend.

The first Blue Goose was initially purchased because Dorothy didn't like to fly, as the Combs family traveled extensively to their winter home in Florida and racetracks throughout the country. The second Blue Goose evolved into a party mobile with seats covered in bright floral fabrics of gold, orange, and green which only added to the playful atmosphere. A visitor arriving on board would probably find Leslie's own personal pillow adorned with Spendthrift's racing colors of blue and orange displayed in an area of prominence stating, "This is my damn bus and I'll do as I damn well please." And out of that potent philosophy, a Thoroughbred racing and breeding dynasty was bred.

CHAPTER TWO

SPENDTHRIFT THE NAMESAKE

Spendthrift Farm's namesake was bred by A.J. Alexander at Woodburn Farm near Midway, Kentucky. Spendthrift, an elegant chestnut adorned with a star and two white hind pasterns, was a foal of 1876 sired by imported Australian out of Aerolite, by Lexington.

Australian was bred in England, and sired by West Australian. He was purchased as a weanling by A. Keene Richards of Blue Grass Farm in Georgetown, Kentucky, and raced in England with moderate success under the name Millington. Australian was purchased by Robert A. Alexander in 1861, the founder of Woodburn, and made one start as a four-year-old for his new owner before retiring to stud alongside the legendary sire Lexington.

Although Lexington received the best mares to his court, Australian was not slighted. The mating between Australian and the Lexington mare Aerolite produced Spendthrift, and the outstanding racehorse Fellowcraft (the damsire of John E. Madden's famous stayer Hamburg) and Mozart, a blind horse that won several races.

Well respected by breeders as a source of classic ability, Australian sired 1877 Kentucky Derby winner Baden-Baden, 1873 Belmont Stakes winner Springbok, and the outstanding broodmare Maggie B.B.

A.J. Alexander, who inherited Woodburn following his brother Robert's death in 1867, sold the Australian-Aerolite colt to Daniel Swigert as a yearling. Swigert named the colt in honor of his wife's outrageous spending sprees to New York. The following year, Mrs. Swigert promptly named Spendthrift's full brother Miser in jest.

The writer Walter Vosburgh described Spendthrift as "a chestnut with a diamond-shaped star, and both hind pasterns white. He had a beautiful clean-cut head, deep neck, short back, and his shoulders were a trifle heavy. He also had very thin-soled feet, and hard ground gave him trouble. He was a fine-tempered horse and easy to ride."

Spendthrift made his racing debut on September 13, 1878, sporting the silks of the Swigert Stable. The going was listed as "wet" which did not deter Spendthrift, as he galloped away to win by four lengths. In the Sanford Stakes at Louisville, Spendthrift cruised to an easy three-length score. The proceeds from the victory were donated to benefit the victims of yellow fever.

In the Young America Stakes at Nashville, Tennessee, Spendthrift scored handily over Lord Murphy, eventual winner of the 1879 Kentucky Derby and another grandson of Lexington. In his final start of the racing season, Spendthrift bettered Lord Murphy over a mile and remained undefeated as a two-year-old.

News of Spendthrift's racing exploits reached New York financier James R. Keene, who offered Swigert $15,000 for the son of Australian. Swigert, who had turned down an offer of $10,000 for the colt from sportsman James Gordon, readily accepted Keene's offer.

Spendthrift, trained by Colonel Thomas Puryear, carried Keene's blue and white spotted silks to a second-place finish behind the highly-touted Dan Sparling in the Withers Stakes, his first defeat. He returned to Belmont Park with a vengeance, and easily won the 1879 Belmont Stakes in 2:42 3/5. Spendthrift further established his credentials as one of the finest three-year-olds in the country with a victory in the Jersey Derby.

The flashy chestnut displayed amazing courage at the start of the Lorillard Stakes (named after prominent breeder and owner Peter Lorillard), when he was accidentally kicked by Magnesium or Harold and left standing at the post 50 yards behind the field as they galloped down the racetrack. Making up ground with amazing tenacity, Spendthrift picked off his opponents one by one, and collared Harold on the lead to post a length victory. The chart called Spendthrift a "dead game colt" that left Harold "staggering."

Spendthrift ran up against one of his toughest rivals in the 1879 Travers Stakes. Falsetto, second to Lord Murphy in the 1879 Derby, was a tough and courageous colt. Spendthrift, whose form was compromised by sore feet on a dry track, was unable to catch Falsetto as he scampered to a two-length score.

The two opponents met again at Saratoga in the Kenner Stakes, and Falsetto bested Spendthrift, whose bruised soles continued to worsen. Spendthrift finished out his three-year-old season with a win in the Champion Stakes at Monmouth Park and a loss at Jerome Park. Although Spendthrift was named the co-champion colt of 1879 along with Falsetto, there was a price to be paid. Spendthrift's feet were in such bad shape that he had to be placed under veterinary care for several months.

Spendthrift's four-year-old campaign was star-crossed from the beginning. The lure of racing in England was just too much for Keene to bypass, and his intent was to send Spendthrift and the good colt Foxhall across the Atlantic.

Foxhall, sound and freshened, was game for travel, but the journey was delayed when Spendthrift continued to be plagued with sore hooves. Within several weeks, he recovered and was sent to England. Foxhall made the journey a profitable one by winning the 1880 Ascot Gold Cup. Spendthrift, however, caught a virus prior to the Cambridgeshire Stakes and finished unplaced in his only start on English soil.

There is a distinct possibility that Spendthrift's wind had been affected by the infection and damp English climate. After being sent home, Spendthrift made two unsuccessful starts as a five-year-old in 1881, and was retired to stud.

Castleton Farm had not yet become a reality for Keene, and Spendthrift was sent to William Kenney's farm near Lexington to stand his first season. The son of Australian stood at Kenney's farm for four years before being sold by Keene after an attempt to capture the wheat market led to his temporary financial ruin.

Spendthrift stood at Dr. E.M. Norwood's farm in Lexington for several years, but was eventually purchased by Senator Johnson N. Camden, Overton, and Christopher Chenault as the Spendthrift Stud partnership. He was sent to Camden's Camden Stud located near Versailles, Kentucky. Following the dissolution of the partnership in 1892, Spendthrift was purchased for $13,000 by Overton Chenault, and spent his final years at Chenault's farm on Winchester Pike on the outskirts of Lexington.

As a sire, Spendthrift is best known as the paternal great grandsire of Man o' War through his son Hastings, the sire of Fair Play. Hastings, foaled in 1893, was a crack three-year-old campaigned by Major August Belmont, who purchased him for $37,000, which was considered an astronomical price at the time.

Hastings was well known for his fiery temperament, which hampered his racing performance on occasion. The game brown colt won the 1896 Belmont Stakes, and three other stakes out of 12 starts. As a sire, he was prolific and consistent, siring such runners as 1898 Kentucky Derby winner and sire Plaudit. Hastings retired to Belmont's Nursery Stud near Lexington, and led the American General Sire list in 1902 and 1904. He died on June 17, 1917, at the age of 24.

Spendthrift also sired the game racehorse and sire Kingston, a winner in 89 of 138 starts, 30 stakes wins, with earnings of $140,195. Kingston, bred by Keene, and his English-bred dam Kapunda were sold for $2,200 to E.V. Snedeker and J.F. Cushman following Keene's financial demise.

Keene eventually recouped his fortune, and repurchased Kingston to stand at his newly-acquired Castleton Farm on Mt. Horeb Pike near Lexington. Kingston did not disappoint as a stallion, leading the American sire list in 1900 and 1910. He died at the ripe old age of 28 at Castleton Farm in 1912.

Spendthrift sired a myriad of great runners during his career, including 1894 Belmont Stakes winner Assignee, 1894 Kentucky Oaks winner Selika, and multiple stakes winners Bankrupt, Lamplighter, Stowaway, and Lazzarone.

The infirmities of old age eventually caught up with Spendthrift, and the grand old warrior died at the age of 24 at Chenault's Spendthrift Stud on October 21, 1900. In Spendthrift's obituary from the

Thoroughbred Record, Chenault fondly accounted the stallion's attributes as if he were an old friend.

"His disposition was superb. I never owned, and never expect to own, a horse with a sweeter disposition. He displayed nothing of the traits which afterward appeared in Hastings, and were later transmitted to a lesser degree to some of his daughters."

CHAPTER THREE

THE MASTER SALESMAN

Saratoga was a stopping point for Leslie Combs as he journeyed to England to watch Crowned Prince, a full brother to 1969 Kentucky Derby winner Majestic Prince, make his initial bow at Newmarket on August 21, 1971. Crowned Prince, bred and consigned by Combs, was sold to Canadian oil and gas millionaire Frank McMahon for a then-world record price of $510,000 at the 1970 Keeneland yearling sales.

"I thought that Majestic Prince was the best colt I ever raised," Combs recalled to *Sports Illustrated* prior to the sale. "But now I've changed my mind. His brother is the best looking young colt I've ever seen. When he comes into the sales ring next summer, it's going to be something. I'm going to announce that McMahon owns half of the dam and further state that both of us may bid. I just want Frank to have his chips ready because old cousin Leslie might wind up buying this colt himself."

McMahon, high on the colt, predicted to Combs that Crowned Prince might rival Majestic Prince in talent.

"They're chockful of hopes for this colt," Combs told *The Morning Telegraph* in 1971. "I'm told that he has already worn out several workmates who are good prospects themselves. McMahon thinks he will be a good one, perhaps better than Majestic Prince. If nothing else, Crowned Prince has the conformation. He was the best looking foal I've ever seen, and he's blossomed into a striking individual."

Crowned Prince developed into a talented juvenile, and was honored as the English champion two-year-old. Although he set a new world record price as a yearling, Crowned Prince was never able to match the racing exploits of Majestic Prince, who became the first member of the family to fetch a then-world record yearling price of $250,000 in 1967.

Combs became a co-founder of the Breeders' Sales Company in 1943 after wartime restrictions kept Kentucky horsemen from sending their sales yearlings by railroad to Saratoga Springs, New York, for the annual sales venue. Combs, and several other breeders with an idea, sold their select yearlings in a tent at Keeneland racecourse.

"That is where we started, in a tent at Keeneland selling our stock," Combs told a newspaper. "A group of breeders got together, and we came up with the idea. It worked, and the select yearling sales were born. The first yearlings I sold were at Saratoga. I got some pretty fair prices for a Menow colt and others."

Leslie Combs, trainer Chrisman, and Louis B. Mayer at the Breeders' Sales in 1950.

Combs became a director of Breeders' Sales Company, which evolved into the sales division for Keeneland. He also served as the secretary-treasurer for the company.

Although Combs had extensive commercial breeding success with a variety of clients, one of his most memorable and lasting relationships evolved with cosmetics entrepreneur Elizabeth (Nightingale) Arden Graham, one of the most successful business women of her time.

Arden wanted to buy horses and Combs offered his assistance because he claimed that "she didn't know a horse from a billy goat."

The longstanding business relationship and friendship between Combs and Graham began in 1944. Combs picked the horses for Arden, and bid on them. In return she would buy one from Spendthrift Farm. It was a dream partnership that provided platinum results. Arden came into the partnership with a horse budget of $3 million, the majority of which was channeled into Spendthrift yearlings.

"I became associated with Elizabeth Arden in the '40s," Combs told the *Thoroughbred Record* in 1967. "Her trainer, Tom Smith, was the only one who really taught me how to look at a racehorse. He said 'Start with the head and take in the whole picture with your eye – his ears, down the tip of his nose, his neck, shoulder, back, right down the hind leg, and he should all fit in a frame, in balance – if he's a good one.'"

Arden, who raced under the nom-de-course of "Mr. Nightingale" prior to changing her stable name to Maine Chance Farm in 1943, had raced horses prior to meeting Combs, but not with the same level of success. In 1945, Maine Chance vaulted to the head of the owners' standings with $589,170 in earnings. The 800 acre "beauty resort" named Maine Chance Farm located on Iron Works Pike in Lexington, was purchased by Arden in 1956. It became a "spa" of sorts, for wealthy women and their entourage. The majority of her horses were boarded at Spendthrift.

Elizabeth Arden Graham and Leslie Combs at Keeneland in 1950.

"Aunt" Elizabeth would never give Dad a monetary limit," said Brownell Combs, reflecting. "She would just tell him which ones to buy upon recommendation. It seems like the horses always worked out for her. She and dad were like old friends from the start. She (Arden) became like family."

The horses worked and then some. At the 1944 Keeneland sales venue, Arthur B. Hancock, Sr., sent two yearlings into the ring at the same time to give the purchaser a choice. Although it is an unheard of practice in this day and age, it was a novel idea in 1944. Conditions declared that the buyer could take home either filly, while Hancock kept the other. One of the fillies was sired by Stimulus out of Risk, and the other was a daughter of Sir Gallahad III. The Risk filly was a half sister to the game Hopeful Stakes winner Sky Larking.

After a final bid of $22,000, Combs selected the Stimulus filly in spite of Arden's declaration to the contrary.

"But Mr. Hancock told me she has splints," Arden whispered to Combs, who held fast to his choice. The clean-legged Sir Gallahad III filly was sold to Fred Hooper privately and named Gallonia. In spite of her good looks, she wasn't much of a racehorse, winning only two of 13 starts for earnings of $4,700.

The Stimulus filly with splints turned out to be Beaugay, named the champion two-year-old filly in 1945 racing under the colors of Maine Chance Farm. Beaugay won six starts in succession, including the Fashion, Polly Drummond, Arlington Lassie, Princess Pat, and Matron Stakes, before bolting through the rail in the Belmont Futurity. Although she never returned to her previous form, Beaugay returned to the racetrack in June of her three-year-old year. She retired in 1948, with nine wins and three seconds from 18 starts.

"With Mrs. Graham, I got along with her right from the start because she doesn't like yes men," Combs recalled in the *Saturday Evening Post*. "When we decided we liked a horse, she'd buy him and never look back. Once in awhile, she'd see one walking down the road and she'd buy him, and by gosh he'd be a runner. She's learned how to pick them."

Arden also purchased Star Pilot in 1944 for $26,000. The following year, he was named champion juvenile colt. That same year she also purchased eventual 1947 Kentucky Derby winner and Spendthrift sire Jet Pilot for $41,000. In 1948, she bought eventual two-year-old champion Myrtle Charm from Combs for $27,000.

Jet Pilot, E. Guerin up, wins the Kentucky Derby in 1947.

"'Aunt' Elizabeth had an amazing amount of success with dad and the horses," said Brownell. "Myrtle Charm was a beautiful mare. She became the champion two-year-old of 1948, and the great grandam of Seattle Slew. An interesting fact surrounding Jet Pilot and Myrtle Charm is that they were both produced from daughters of Spendthrift's foundation mares Myrtlewood and Black Curl, who were half sisters out of Frizeur."

Jet Pilot was produced by Black Wave, a daughter of Black Curl sired by *Sir Gallahad III. He also retired to stud at Spendthrift.

Myrtle Charm, out of Myrtlewood's daughter Crepe Myrtle, won five of eight starts as a two-year-old, including the 1948 Spinaway and Matron Stakes, and the Arlington Matron Handicap.

Arden and Combs shared a sense of humor along with their passion for fine horses. Arden once sent a supply of beauty cream down from New York to Spendthrift, and instructed Combs that the cream could only be used on her horses to heal cuts.

"We tried it," Combs told the *Saturday Evening Post*. "We found out it was one of the best things you can use. Now that her horses are no longer here (at Spendthrift), I'm still using it on my own – and I have to buy it."

Combs' success as a commercial breeder turned the yearling sales into a big business venture with an essence of southern charm that lured not only Wall Street financiers, movie moguls, and cosmetic entrepreneurs, but movie stars as well. Spendthrift's famous parties leading up to the summer sales became well-known as a playground for the rich and famous. The Keeneland summer sale became the social event of the season not to be missed. It was not unusual to see women wearing fur in July, and men sporting ascots as they stepped out of their Rolls Royce, and handed their keys to the Keeneland valet.

"Our house was always full of entertainers around sale time. I remember Fred Astaire tap dancing down to dinner," recalled Brownell. "How about that. It was quite something to see. I was just a little guy, but who could forget Fred Astaire? We always seemed to have a movie star or two staying at the house during the sales."

The prestigious list of Spendthrift clients included George D. Widener, chairman of the Jockey Club; Captain Harry F. Guggenheim of Cain Hoy Stable; Christopher J. Devine, Wall Street bond broker; entrepreneur Louis Wolfson; publishers John Knight and Marshall Field; Lord Derby; Texas oil baron Ralph Lowe; and Mrs. Norman Woolworth.

From 1949 through 1964, in 1967, and in 1972, Spendthrift headed the list as the leading consignor at the Keeneland July Selected Yearling Sale. In 1964, Spendthrift held the highest sales average on record with six yearlings sold for an average of $67,667. That same year, Combs set a new world record at Keeneland for a broodmare sold at auction when the Princequillo mare La Dauphine, a daughter of Baby League in foal to Bold Ruler, was purchased by Charles Wacker for $177,000.

Combs became the first commercial breeder to gross more than $1 million at a single sale in 1967, with 28 yearlings selling for

$1,181,500, and an average of $42,196. That same year, Combs became the first market breeder to surpass the $1 million mark with $1,190,470 generated from Spendthrift-bred runners. In 1972, Combs surpassed his own record once again as America's leading consignor, with 29 Spendthrift yearlings sold for $1,733,500. He also became the first commercial breeder to sell two eventual champions in Myrtle Charm and Idun.

Everett Clay, a close friend and associate of Combs from Miami, Florida, told the *Lexington Herald-Leader* that Combs was a master salesman with "a soft sell and an uncanny ability to touch the hidden persuader which unleashes the desire to own and possess something rare and priceless."

Although Combs possessed the talent of an ingenious salesman, at times it was difficult for him to overcome the shyness he possessed as a child.

"I'm still so shy that if I know you're going to buy yearlings, but I don't know you, then it's going to be difficult for me to walk up to you, and try to push you into buying a horse," he said.

Haden Kirkpatrick, a friend of Combs and a former owner and editor of the *Thoroughbred Record* stated that, "Leslie could pick up that phone any morning and raise $1 million by nightfall without even telling them (the buyers) what the horse is."

Combs established his reputation with hard work and integrity. A Spendthrift yearling sold for $25,000 and developed a swelling on its leg following the sale. According to the disgruntled buyer, the colt had been kicked on its way back from the sales ring. Combs bought the colt back without issue. That was the type of integrity that ensured Spendthrift's rise to the top.

The 3P's of equine marketing – performance, prestige, and pedigree – were one of the hard and fast rules utilized by Combs in promoting sales yearlings.

"Spendthrift yearlings carry the blood of champions," Combs told the *Lexington Herald-Leader* in 1968. "They are sired by champion stallions, and are out of mares which have won stakes or have already produced the winners of blue ribbon stakes races. People tell me that

Spendthrift yearlings have become status symbols, like jewelry. We sell what we have done in the past, and the record speaks for itself. You breed the best to the best, and that's what we do."

In 1956, Combs consigned nine yearlings to the Keeneland summer yearling sale, and established a record average of $40,232 for a consignment. Included in that group of yearlings was eventual two-year-old filly champion Idun, purchased for a then-record $63,000 by Josephine Paul.

According to an article in the *Lexington Herald Leader*, Paul revealed her exuberance over the purchase of Idun following her championship juvenile career when she jumped up at a luncheon and announced enthusiastically as Combs entered the room, "There's the man who sold me Idun!" Combs just smiled.

Combs' first world-record yearling sold was a chestnut colt sired by Swaps out of Obedient. The plucky youngster sold for $130,000 at the 1961 Keeneland summer venue to buyer John Olin. The colt was named Swapson, and won several races in the United States and Venezuela. He retired with career earnings of $26,766.

"It's amazing what people will pay for a piece of the pie," Combs said following the sale in July 1961. "The colt was beautiful, just like his daddy. We expect to see big things out of that fella.'"

In 1965, a Bold Ruler colt named One Bold Bid became the new record holder when Velma Morrison purchased him for $170,000 from Spendthrift's consignment at the summer sales.

The following year, the partnership of Combs and Charles Wacker III consigned a yearling son of Bold Ruler out of Le Dauphine to the Keeneland Summer Sale. The colt was purchased by Frank McMahon for a new world-record price of $200,000.

"See, I didn't let it get me down," Combs told the *Lexington Leader* in 1966. "If you've got the goods people will pay for them. This was a tremendous colt. We figured with his credentials and bloodlines the youngster had an excellent chance of surpassing the previous (sales record) mark, and he did."

The colt was named Bold Discovery, and never recouped his purchase price on the racetrack. He made four starts as a three-year-old and never won a race.

The next duo of world-record-priced yearlings were full brothers, and well worth their purchase price. The 1967 headliner was 1969 Kentucky Derby winner Majestic Prince, purchased for $250,000 by McMahon.

The following year, Crowned Prince stole the spotlight with McMahon writing the check for more than double the cost of Majestic Prince. Crowned Prince, an English champion, eventually became a successful sire and the fifth-leading broodmare sire in England in 1988.

Combs once again topped the sale for the fifth time in 1974 with the world-record-priced full brother to Mr. Prospector named Kentucky Gold. The bay colt, purchased for $625,000 by Mr. and Mrs. Wallace Gilroy, became a minor winner and earned only $5,950.

The last full sibling to Majestic Prince and Crowned Prince became Combs' final world-record-priced yearling in 1975. Elegant Prince was purchased by Mr. and Mrs. Franklin Groves for $715,000. He never started and died in 2000.

Unlike many Thoroughbred breeders of the time, Combs sent the best colts and fillies produced by Spendthrift to the select yearling sales.

"I race a few fillies only," Combs told *Sports Illustrated* in 1969. "I keep them for breeding purposes. The reason I don't race any of my colts is that I could be criticized for trying to keep the best stock for myself instead of putting it in the sales. For the same reason I don't sell privately. Everything is for sale. The best go in the Keeneland Summer Sales. Any of the leftovers passed over in the fall sale, would I consider selling privately? That doesn't happen often."

Combs freely gave advice to the new buyer or curious reporter investigating the Spendthrift recipe for success, and summarized it by immediately referring back to the obvious conclusion.

"I tell him to buy colts if he is primarily interested in racing, but to buy fillies if he wants to breed later," Combs stated. "I suggest that he (the new buyer) hit the middle of the price range, the $50,000 to $100,000 range, because that is where you get your best money value.

"When I say it will cost you $1 million to get into racing sensibly, I'm looking at it realistically, too. You should have a four-year program and plan to spend $200,000 a year buying. Buy five yearlings – three fillies and two colts – for each of the four years. At the end of the four years you will have spent $800,000 on purchases, plus another $200,000 on boarding and training fees, etc, and you will own eight colts and 12 fillies, half of whom will have had ample chance to show you what they can do on the racetrack. The point is, if you've spent your money wisely you will either have won your investment out or have more than $1 million in value. Now you can't walk into places like Darby Dan or Greentree and buy well-bred stock. These people breed to race, not to sell. That leaves you out in the cold. Logic says you should do your buying at Spendthrift."

Chapter Four

THE GREAT SYNDICATOR

When movie mogul and California Thoroughbred breeder Louis B. Mayer decided he was going to sell all his racing and breeding stock, it became the sales event of the season. With all the trappings of a movie premier, over 7,000 spectators and bidders flowed into Santa Anita racetrack for the sale on February 27, 1947. By the end of the evening 60 horses in training had been sold for a then-record $1,553,500, with an average of $25,891.

Mayer, who was the second-ranked breeder in 1947 with his horses earning $1,277,377, sold his entire stable over the next several years. By 1950, Mayer's Thoroughbred assets had been dispersed – either by auction or sold privately – for an aggregate $4,479,650. Included in the private sales were the purchase and syndication of Beau Pere and Alibhai to Leslie Combs.

Beau Pere, a moderate winner in England, was a foal of 1927 sired by Son-in-Law out of One Thousand Guineas-winner Cinna. He retired to stud in Newmarket, and failed to attract much interest due to his lack of race record. He was sold and exported to New Zealand, where he became a champion sire in that country and Australia. Beau Pere did leave a lasting impression in American pedigrees as the sire of Iron Reward, the dam of Swaps, and Flower Bed, the granddam of the popular Kentucky stallion Graustark.

Alibhai never made it to the racetrack. Bred in England, he was sired by the great Hyperion out of Goodwood Cup winner Teresina, who was placed in the Oaks and the St. Leger. Exported to the United States as a yearling, Alibhai showed great promise while in training, but injured both sesamoids and was retired to stud prematurely. In spite of his unsoundness, Alibhai became a leading stallion in the United States, and sired 1954 Kentucky Derby winner Determine – the sire of 1962 Kentucky Derby winner Decidedly, and Your Host – the sire of 1960-61 Horse of the Year Kelso.

"When I returned to Kentucky in 1937," Combs recalled in a 1966 interview with the *Morning Telegraph*, "I tried to breed the few mares that I had purchased to some top studs. I couldn't do it because they were closed corporations for the most part, owned by one or two people who either traded seasons to close friends, or who had enough mares to keep their stallions busy. It was tough going for a number of years."

After a failed attempt to get a mare to the popular stallion Sir Gallahad III, Combs realized that a new plan was in order.

"I went to Bull Hancock's dad and told him I had a stakes mare which I wanted to breed to Sir Gallahad III," said Combs. "But seasons to Sir Gallahad III, the nation's leading stallion, were hard to come by – especially for a young, unestablished fellow like me. Mr. Hancock tried to sell me a season to other less desirable stallions. Right then and there I knew the only way to get ahead would be to acquire my own stallions, and then I recalled what had been done in England – syndication – where several owners share the risk."

Combs' decision to syndicate stallions was a brilliant one. Although he did not originate this form of partial ownership, Combs recognized the value of spreading the risk and the investment in an attempt to make a stallion. The repositioning of stallion syndication also helped launch the emphasis of producing a sales product. Instead of promoting the female family and the stallion's siblings, the sire's race record and those of his offspring came to the forefront as a promotional tool. It also provided for bloodline diversity by creating a larger pool of mares to draw from for a stallion's book.

Prior to syndicating Beau Pere, Combs contacted the British Bloodstock Agency and asked if he could have copies of their syndication forms to use as a prototype. His stallion syndication forms contained only four pages, unlike the modern syndication agreements which are lengthy in comparison. Combs also consistently sold 32 shares per stallion. The syndication concept not only helped to spread the risk, but also to reap the rewards. Each owner of a syndicate share had a seasonal breeding right for one mare to that stallion each year, unless the agreement carried a clause for a bonus year (two mares per season) which was available to certain stallions. As a result, the board, advertising, and veterinary bills were spread among all members of the syndicate, who still retained the right to profit from the stallion's offspring each year without bearing the entire cost of stallion ownership. The stallion's book was closed to outside breeders, unless a shareholder's season or share came up for sale, which had to be approved by the syndicate manager before the transaction could be made.

"This way," Combs said in a 1960 interview with the *Saturday Evening Post*, "A man can own shares in several stallions, instead of putting all his money into one. Let's stick to round numbers. (An estimate) of 30 stud fees at $10,000 each comes back to $300,000 a year. Now I multiply by four. You must have your money back in four years, because the horse might not be a successful stallion. You can't tell until his produce run as three-year-olds, and that's four years after you've started him at stud. Well, four times $300,000 is $1,200,000. So you should be in the clear at the end of the fourth year."

Combs altered the syndication process by not just looking for people with top mares but with money. He also formed syndicates of 10-15 investors rather than the old fashioned way of just including three or four friends in on the deal. Combs secured many syndication agreements over the phone before any paperwork was completed.

"There were many times I'd watch him (Combs) syndicate horses on the phone...nothing written, not even a handshake," recalled Combs' son-in-law David Trapp in an interview with the *Courier-Journal* in 1990.

The *Thoroughbred Record* wrote in 1968 that "Mr. Combs may properly be said to have taken the already-existing idea of syndication and brought it in practice to such a degree of perfection as to approach an art."

Beau Pere became the first stallion and first failure to be syndicated by Combs. He was syndicated into 15 shares divided in partnership with the likes of Hal Price Headley, Warren Wright of Calumet Farm, and his uncle Brownell. Beau Pere, purchased for $100,000 at the age of 20, died within two months of arriving at Spendthrift. He never covered a mare.

"That taught me one thing," Combs said in a 1962 interview with *Turf and Sport Digest*. "It is too risky to move a horse that is well past middle age."

Undaunted, Combs plunged back into the well and pulled out Alibhai.

"The Dude, Cover Up, and Solidarity were racing about that time, and Alibhai was acquiring a fine reputation," Combs told the *Thoroughbred Record* in 1964. "Everybody said I was making a big mistake, but I offered Mayer $500,000 for Alibhai and he accepted. Incidently that was quite a lot of money for a stallion at that time. Mayer was wonderful to me, perhaps out of regret for my unfortunate experience with Beau Pere. After agreeing to our price, he later received an offer of $550,000 from another group, but refused to renege on the original deal. And when I got back home and found I could only sell 20 of the proposed 30 shares, he told me not to worry, that he would take the rest."

After the loss of Beau Pere, investors were less than enthusiastic about entering into another syndication agreement, and especially one involving an unraced horse. After being informed of Combs' ailing syndication, Mayer re-entered the picture and purchased a one-third interest in 10-year-old Alibhai. The original investors did not regret their decision. After Combs announced that the initial 30 shares in Alibhai were sold, he was overwhelmed by requests for shares and was able to disperse Mayer's remaining interest easily. At Spendthrift, Alibhai became one of the most successful unraced stallions in Thoroughbred history as the sire of over 50 stakes winners, and has remained an influential aspect in modern pedigrees.

"Alibhai, that was a lucky break," Combs recalled in an interview. "After the flop of Beau Pere, anything would have been an improvement, but Alibhai was an absolute winner."

Following the success of Alibhai, Combs purchased *Royal Charger with the help of Irish attorney Neil McCarthy from the Irish National Stud. The $300,000 sale of the highly successful stallion had ignited a debate with the Irish Parliament after horsemen and the press determined that the sale had been a serious loss to the Irish breeding industry. Royal Charger was deemed an Irish national treasure, and

Combs even turned down $1 million from an Irish syndicate for the horse. The press had been correct in their assumption. Royal Charger went on to sire such outstanding get as *Turn-to, Royal Native, Idun, Royal Orbit, and Royal Serenade, and became the maternal grandsire of two-time Claiborne-bred champion Gamely through his daughter Gambetta. The brilliant son of Nasrullah has remained an important influence in modern pedigrees.

Combs' determination paid off again after securing the purchase of *My Babu from the wife of Pratapsingh Gaekwar, the Maharajah of Baroda, for $650,000 in 1955. The Maharajah initially purchased the Two Thousand Guineas winner from his trainer and breeder, Peter Beatty and the Aga Kahn, and wasn't game to sell in the beginning. However, when the Maharani and Maharajah decided to divorce, she received the horses as part of the settlement and sold My Babu to Spendthrift Farm.

My Babu at Spendthrift after his arrival from Ireland in 1955.

"I tried for more than seven years before I was able to get My Babu for Spendthrift Farm," Combs recalled in an interview with *Turf and Sport Digest* in 1962. "My first interest was when Fred Armstrong was training him for the Maharajah. I was impressed by the horse's bloodlines and his racing. I wanted him when he retired to stud over there, and wanted him even more after the way his progeny ran."

The son of Djebel was purchased sight unseen by Combs, who expressed satisfaction when My Babu walked off the airplane at Bluegrass Field in Lexington in 1955.

"I'm seeing the horse for the first time today," Combs told a reporter as he examined My Babu. "I'm highly pleased with him. Look at him walk into that van like he owned it! That horse has plenty of sense... I like him."

My Babu topped the leading sire list of two-year-olds by money won in England (1958), France (1959) and America (1960). He stood at Spendthrift for eight years before his exportation to Ireland in 1963, and eventually to Japan.

Jockey Bill Shoemaker said that Gallant Man was the best distance horse he had ever ridden shortly after the son of Migoli set a new American record of 2:26 3/5 for 1 1/2 miles in the 1957 Belmont Stakes. It was a well-heeled statement at best, considering that Shoemaker's lack of judgement caused Gallant Man to lose the 1957 Kentucky Derby by a nose to Iron Liege. Shoemaker misjudged the finish line and stood up in the stirrups too early, slowing Gallant Man's drive to the wire, which allowed Iron Liege to put a nose in front.

In spite of the Derby blunder, the talented runner amassed earnings of $510,355 with 14 wins, four seconds, and one third out of 26 starts. His only bit of hard luck in an otherwise stellar career was having been foaled in the same year as Bold Ruler and Round Table, who collected honors as 1958 champion sprinter and handicap horse, respectively, that year.

Combs showed an interest in purchasing Gallant Man after watching him win the 1957 Hibiscus Stakes at Hialeah Park, but bided his time as the colt's form continued to improve. Gallant Man retired due to a painful reoccurring splint in the left foreleg, and Combs formed a syndicate and approached owner Ralph Lowe about purchasing the horse. Lowe sold a three-quarter interest in the successful stakes winner to Combs for $1 million in September, 1958. Standing a mere 15.1 hands tall, Gallant Man sired a string of successful stakes winners and became highly regarded as a broodmare sire.

Gallant Man stood at Spendthrift throughout the entirety of his career, and died in 1988 at the age of 34. When the plucky bay stallion passed away, his former trainer John Nerud recalled, "When he was sound and good, a horse never lived who could beat him...he had it all – speed and endurance."

In all, Combs syndicated a dozen horses for $1 million or better: Gallant Man ($1,333,333 in 1958), Bald Eagle ($1,400,000 in 1960); Never Bend ($1,225,000 in 1964, Fleet Nasrullah ($1,050,000 in 1965), Creme Dela Creme ($1,200,000 in 1966), Raise a Native ($2,625,000 in 1967), Majestic Prince ($1,800,000 in 1970), Unconscious ($1,800,000 in 1971), Exclusive Native ($1,920,000 in 1972), Kennedy Road ($1,444,000 in 1973), and Cornish Prince ($1,200,000 in 1972).

"Quality mares are the foundation of a great stud farm," Combs said. "But the stallions are your bread and butter. You better have a great one, several good ones, and a few moderate ones to keep the salt on the table."

Leslie's son, Brownell Combs, was responsible for the creation of many successful syndications. Brownell was named Spendthrift's general manager in 1974 after Leslie, bordering on retirement, handed over all business operations of the farm to his son. Brownell, managing Spendthrift along with his wife, Linda, updated the farm operations while maintaining Spendthrift's old-world traditions.

Brownell organized the world-record syndication of Affirmed for $14 million in 1978, Seattle Slew for $12 million, Wajima for a then-record $7.2 million in 1975, the $3.24 million syndication of Sham in 1973, and the $4.6 million syndication of leading French sire Caro (Ire) in 1978. Brownell wrote his own stallion syndication agreements, which were much more detailed and lengthy in comparison to his father's succinct four-page contracts. He also increased the number of shares sold to 45.

"The Thoroughbred industry had changed," Brownell recalled. "You had to run it more like a corporation, and cover every base. It was more complicated. My father did things with a phone call and a handshake – it was outdated. It wasn't unusual for us to write a 45-page stallion syndication agreement. Times demanded change. John Gaines (of Gainesway Farm) was increasing the book to 40-plus mares to his stallions, and we had to keep up."

Brownell's accomplishments gained little praise, if any, from his father. Like many entrepreneurs, whose blood and sweat founded a dynasty, Combs had a difficult time relinquishing his hold over Spendthrift Farm.

Combs could sometimes sound jealous of Brownell's accomplishments, and periodically second-guessed his son's decisions regarding the farm. If Brownell was called "Mr. Combs" in Leslie's presence, he immediately corrected the faux pas. "There ain't but one Mr. Combs," he would say and point to his son. "That's Brownell."

Multiple Grade 1 winner Wajima, campaigned by East West Stables, was syndicated into 36 shares at $200,000 per share. Twenty shares were retained by the owners, and the remaining 16 were sold

Brownell Combs with Multiple Grade 1 winner Wajima.

privately. Wajima is best known for his four consecutive Grade 1 wins in the Monmouth Invitational, the Travers Stakes, The Governors, and the Marlboro Cup, and a gutsy second-place finish to Forego in the Woodward Stakes.

Caro, winner of the 1970 Poule d'Essai Poulains and the Prix d'Ispahan, made a dramatic impact in France by siring Group 1 winner Theia in his first crop in 1975. His second crop was no less distinguished with the likes of Group 1 winners Carwhite, Crystal Palace, and Madelia. Caro had become an international sensation, and had outgrown the limitations of standing in France. The conclusion was to find an American buyer. Spendthrift Farm stepped forward, and Caro was sent to Kentucky from his home at Haras du Bois Roussel in September, 1977.

The crisis which occurred following Caro's importation was nothing short of disaster.

On September 9, after Caro had left France, the United States Department of Agriculture placed an embargo on importing horses from Ireland, Britain, and France. The USDA had picked up reports of a highly-contagious equine venereal disease causing rampant early abortions in the aforementioned countries. The French, British, and Irish seemed unconcerned following a USDA inquiry. The French even stated that they could certify horses being sent to the United States as disease-free. The USDA sent a team of inspectors to Europe, and discovered the venereal disease was contagious equine metritis (CEM), which is so highly contagious it can be transmitted by handlers having contact with an infected horse.

"My (then) wife Linda (Combs) secured the transaction," Brownell recalled. "She was instrumental in the purchase of Caro, which we bought for a song from the French. She was a heck of a business woman, and told the Societe de Encouragement (French Jockey Club) that money wouldn't change hands until the horse was on the plane and in the air. Well, the deal got done, and Caro was on his way to Kentucky along with a little friend he brought with him. The horse was in the air hours before the embargo took effect."

CEM appeared in Kentucky in March, 1978, as the first United States outbreak of the disease. The two most recently-imported stallions from France, Caro and Gainesway Farm-based Lyphard, tested positive for CEM. Both stallions had received clean health certificates from France and had passed the basic USDA testing procedure. A determined search revealed three other infected stallions at Gainesway, and 21 mares located at various farms.

"We were very unpopular there for awhile," Brownell mused. "But we had no idea that Caro was carrying a venereal disease. He had passed all the tests in France, which were obviously bunk. Luckily, the disease was easy to cure, and we got it under control very quickly. Other than the 1978 season, breeders never backed off Caro again. He was a very important importation, and made a great impact on the American breeding scene."

Caro's importation caused a major crisis for the Kentucky breeding industry.

In response to the outbreak, Brownell Combs and Gainesway Farm's owner John Gaines shut down their respective breeding sheds. Spendthrift and Gainesway were losing hundreds of thousands of dollars per day, but it didn't stop members of the Thoroughbred elite from passing the blame.

"They haven't got to the stage of throwing rocks through our windows yet, but they sure are calling and holding lynch meetings," Leslie Combs told *Time Magazine* in 1978. There's no way we would knowingly do anything that would be detrimental to the breeding industry. We've been condemned, and we shouldn't be."

By early April 1978, the CEM outbreak was under control. Kentucky lifted a ban on the in-state shipment of horses, and the embargo on out-of-state horses expired on April 14. Caro and Lyphard were treated for CEM, and went on to become successful American sires. In spite of the losses and frustration, the finality had a positive outcome. The USDA implemented more strict CEM testing and quarantine on all imported horses that remains in place to this day.

Leslie Combs was also responsible for syndicating such successful stallions as Turn-to, Tom Fool, Prince John, Tudor Minstrel, Arctic Prince, Jet Pilot, Seaneen, Solar Slipper, Warfare, Ardan, and Irish Lancer, among many. One of Combs' most celebrated syndications had all the essential ingredients for a mystery novel. The outcome linked together a murder and a match race between America's two most celebrated runners – Swaps and Nashua – which would change the future of stallion syndication forever.

Chapter Five

SWAPS FOR NASHUA

With hawk-like precision, Leslie Combs flew to Chicago in August, 1955, to watch the match race between America's two most celebrated horses of the time, Swaps and Nashua. His intent was to offer owner-breeder Rex Ellsworth $1 million for the purchase of Swaps regardless of the outcome of the race.

The Nashua-Swaps rivalry was akin to that between 1978 Triple Crown winner Affirmed and Alydar, although it was more of an East versus West debate. The two horses were highly talented racehorses, and vastly different in ability and soundness. Bred in Kentucky by William Woodward Jr.'s Belair Stud, Nashua raced predominantly in the East, while California-bred Swaps dominated the Western circuit.

Nashua, a stout and feisty bay son of Nasrullah, out of Segula, by Johnstown, had the physique of a prize fighter and talent to burn. At the culmination of his juvenile season, Nashua was the two-year-old champion with six wins and two seconds from eight starts. He returned the following year to notch divisional honors as champion three-year-old and the coveted Horse of the Year title for owner William Woodward Jr. and legendary trainer Sunny Jim Fitzsimmons.

Swaps was a true California boy and loved to show off for the crowd. A blazing red chestnut with near flawless balance and conformation, Swaps was sired by Khaled out of Iron Reward, by the ill-fated Beau Pere. When he retired to stud in 1956, the brilliant racer held five world records. As a two-year-old Swaps won three of six starts, and returned as a three-year-old to capture the Kentucky Derby by 1 1/2 lengths over Nashua among his eight victories that year. However, Nashua redeemed himself with a one-length tally in the Preakness Stakes and a nine-length win in the Belmont. As a four-year-old, Swaps' brilliance continued with eight wins from 10 starts. He retired with divisional honors as champion handicap horse and Horse of the Year.

The publicity surrounding the Nashua-Swaps match race touted the two horses as athletic celebrities, and covered each and every detail of the preparation of all the personalities involved. It was the media event of the season.

Swaps had been plagued with a stone bruise prior to the race, and trainer Meshach Tenney had cut away a piece of the hoof, packed it with medication, and limited his training regimen. The bruise agitated the champion during the week of the match race, and after consulting with Ellsworth they decided that a postponement was in order. However, it was too late to cancel the race, and a decision was reached not to mention the hoof condition to jockey Bill Shoemaker in case it affected his riding performance.

The outcome of the match race was best described by writer Evan Shipman in his account in the 1956 *American Racing Manual*; "There was nothing complicated about it. As the doors opened, Arcaro, yelling like a banshee and wielding his whip with all his strength, shot Nashua to the front, while Swaps on the way outside, veered farther out toward the outside rail. Nashua was in front as they passed the stand, and he was able to be in front for the entire distance, Swaps making repeated thrusts, all of them falling short."

Nashua won by a convincing 6 1/2 lengths in 2:04 1/5 for the 1 1/4 miles over a good track.

The Swaps camp announced that the great horse was going to rest for the season. Combs was not deterred by the loss. He prodded and pressed Ellsworth to sell Swaps, but to no avail.

Nashua made his next start in the Sysonby Stakes at Belmont Park on September 24, and finished a disappointing third to High Gun. On October 15, Nashua posted a five-length win in the Jockey Club Gold Cup at Belmont, and within two weeks his owner would be found murdered.

New York socialites Woodward and his wife, Ann, were among 58 guests that attended a party for the visiting Duchess of Windsor on October 30 at the Locust Valley Estate of Edith Baker, a banker's widow.

Guests at the party discussed the rash of burglaries in the North Shore area of Long Island. Woodward had a few drinks while Ann mingled, and they left for their Oyster Bay Cove estate around 1 a.m.

Upon arriving at home, the Woodwards retired to separate bedrooms which were located across the hall on the first floor of the home. Due to the wave of burglaries, both had taken to sleeping with weapons by their bed. For Woodward it was a revolver, for Ann a double barrel 12-gauge shotgun.

At approximately 3 a.m. Ann was awakened by the barking of her dog, and heard sounds in the hallway. Fearing that it may have been a prowler, she turned on a night light, grabbed the gun, and flung open the door to her bedroom. The light was dim, and she spotted a figure standing in the doorway of her husband's bedroom. Without making a sound, Ann fired two blasts of the shotgun at the shadowy outline. After it was too late, she realized that she had not shot a prowler, but her husband in a moment of mistaken identity.

When the police arrived on the scene, Woodward, nude, was found dead adjacent to his bedroom. He had been shot in the head and face by the first round, and the second blast had shattered the bedroom door. Ann told police that her husband probably heard the same noise that she had, and had gotten up to investigate. Interestingly enough, the Woodward's children, William and James, slept through the gunfire.

The media circus fed on all the elements of wealth, intrigue, and mystery surrounding the shooting. Was it an accident or murder? A private detective hired by Ann had tracked Woodward's alleged liaisons with other women for a period of seven years. Woodward's relatives had frowned upon his marriage to Ann, a former actress and model, stating that she was merely a social climber.

At some point during the investigation, police discovered a witness who supported Ann's burglary story, and stated that he was in the Woodward mansion at the time of the shooting.

Paul Wirths, arrested for a different burglary in the area, told police that he was in the house, heard the shot, and went out a window to hide in a barn. He also said that he had broken a tree limb when climbing into the Woodward mansion, which was supported by police discovery.

Three weeks after the shooting, Ann appeared before a grand jury and gave testimony that lasted a mere 25 minutes. She was cleared of any wrongdoing, and moved on into the social whirl.

Horses seemed to hold little interest for Ann. Following the death of Woodward, the Hanover Bank, named as executors of his estate, put the esteemed Thoroughbreds of Belair Stud up for sale by sealed bid.

Nashua, who was listed in Group A of the horses offered for sealed bid, was listed by Hanover Bank as "Nashua, b.c., 1952 by Nasrullah – Segula, by Johnstown, 1955 Horse of the Year. Winner at two and three of 16 races and $945,415, including the Belmont Park Juvenile, Grand Union Hotel, Hopeful, Futurity, Flamingo, Wood Memorial, Dwyer, Preakness, Belmont Stakes, Florida Derby, Arlington Classic, Washington Park Match Race, Jockey Club Gold Cup, etc. Nashua is now located at Claiborne Farm, Paris, Kentucky, Telephone Paris 393, where he may be inspected by arrangement with Mr. A.B. Hancock, Jr. He is offered under the following special conditions. 1. A veterinary examination of Nashua will be made by Drs. Hagyard, Davidson, and McGee. Certificate of the horse's soundness for racing purposes will be available for inspection at Claiborne Farm and the Hanover Bank, New York. 2. No examination with respect to Nashua's fertility has ever been made, and none will be made for the purpose of this sale; the executors make no representation as to Nashua's potential ability as a stallion, the horse being offered as he stands."

On December 8, 1955, Dr. Charles E. Hagyard of Hagyard, Davidson, and McGee veterinarians of Lexington, Kentucky, reported his findings to the Hanover Bank after examining Nashua.

"My findings are as follows: Nashua is racing sound and in good health and condition. He has a small non-active splint just below his left knee. This has been present throughout his racing career, and has never troubled him. Sincerely, Charles E. Hagyard, B.V.Sc."

Combs received a telephone call from Christopher J. Devine, a prominent broker on Wall Street, who suggested purchasing Nashua and several other Belair Thoroughbreds. The two men had never met, but Devine had an interest in breeding and boarded his mares at Spendthrift. Combs put in a phone call to his partner John Hanes, who was also enthusiastic over the possibility of purchasing Nashua.

Nashua with Al Robertson, Sunny Jim Fitzsimmons and Leslie Combs.

Via conference call, the three investors – Combs in Lexington, Devine in New Jersey, and Hanes in Long Island – came to an agreement of $1,851,200 for the package deal of Nashua ($1,251,200), the Woodward mares ($400,000), and racing stable ($200,000.) The threesome added an extra $1,200 to the Nashua offer just in case someone bid a higher amount on the package.

"I had a feeling we'd get that damn horse," Combs said in a 1960 interview with the *Saturday Evening Post*, "because I wanted him more than I'd ever wanted any horse. Then the call came. I picked up the phone and one of the vice presidents of the bank said 'you've got him.'"

After Combs hung up the phone, he immediately called Warren Wright, Jr., son of the founder of Calumet Farm and a partner with Combs in an insurance agency, who immediately called Lloyd's of London to purchase insurance for the famous horse.

Although the bid on the mares was off by $15,000, the partnership purchased Nashua for the initial offer, which was $20,000 higher than the next bid. Devine owned a half interest, while Combs and Hanes each owned a quarter. Combs, as the head of the syndicate, sold 32 shares in the son of Nasrullah at approximately $39,000 per share within 10 days of Nashua's purchase. Although the price of over $1 million was unheard of for a horse in the 1950s, Nashua proved well worth the investment.

"We wanted Nashua not only as a racehorse, but as a stud," Combs said in a newspaper interview. "I wanted him as an outcross for the daughters and granddaughters of Myrtlewood. But remember, I have numerous other good ones (mares) that should nick perfectly with Nashua."

The total amount for the 62 Belair Horses, including Nashua, realized $1,866,200. Nashua's dam, Segula, was purchased along with 23 broodmares and 14 yearlings by Mildred Woolwine of White Oaks Farm, formerly part of E.R. Bradley's Idle Hour Farm, in Lexington. When recalling the formation of the original syndicate, Combs reflected with amusement, "Some of those people told me 'Don't mention my name. Let everybody think you're the damn fool paying that much for a horse.'"

In later years, Combs reflected on the simplicity of his early syndication agreements, and compared them with the intricacy of the modern documents.

"I used to take the phone there and syndicate a horse in two hours," Combs told the *Courier-Journal* in 1980. "My contracts were two pages. Now it takes 45 pages for a syndicate agreement. I had clients like Harry Guggenheim, George Widener, the Whitneys. I'd call them and they'd say 'Yeah, I'll take a share. Fine.' Warren Wright. People like that I didn't have any trouble with."

Nashua carried the orange and blue silks of Spendthrift Farm to victory in six of 10 starts during his four-year-old campaign, including the 1956 editions of the Widener and Monmouth Handicaps.

Following Nashua's victory in the Widener, Combs enthusiastically told a reporter, "He stood a terrific drive. I thought he could do it but you never know. It was a great finish. Eddie Arcaro rode a great race, a perfect race. Everybody was shooting for Nashua."

Nashua retired to Spendthrift after scoring his second win in the Jockey Club Gold Cup by 2 1/4 lengths, with an overall record of 22 wins and four seconds from 30 starts. Nashua's career earnings of $1,288,565 surpassed the previous all-time earnings mark set by Citation with a career total of $1,085,760. Nashua was inducted into the National Museum of Racing and Hall of Fame in 1965.

As prolific in the breeding shed as on the racetrack, Nashua sired 77 stakes winners before passing away in 1981 at the ripe old age of 29. The statue of Nashua and his personable groom Clem Brooks resides in the center of the lawn near the U-shaped stallion barn.

Brooks, an astute "stallion man," was Nashua's groom throughout his stud career. A highly-regarded horseman, it was said that Brooks "concentrates totally on the horse in the breeding shed. Never takes his eye off the stallion. There can be all kinds of commotion going on, the mare can squeal and kick and flip, or whatever, the place can catch fire, and Clem never takes his eyes off the horse." The personable and outspoken Brooks enjoyed entertaining the visitors that flocked to see Nashua at Spendthrift. He was the consummate showman, not so unlike his boss Leslie Combs.

"I've had as many as 17 busloads of people in here at once," Brooks recalled in a 1981 interview with Arnold Kirkpatrick. "Seventeen busloads, and I treat 'em all nice."

As Nashua posed regally, Clem would tell the tale of the great horse as the visitors listened intently.

"Ladies and Gentlemen, this is Nashua. The 18th of May, 1956, is when he became the leading money winner of the world. This horses has won one-million, two-hundred and eighty-eight thousand, five hundred and sixty-five dollars...an no cents. He started 30 times, won 22 out of 30, and he was only out of the money twice. His last race was two miles at Belmont Park. He won it and broke the world's record doin' it."

"Back in the days when I first got Nashua, people wanted to buy his shoes, and Mr. Combs claims I'd just sell 'em anything," Brooks recalled to Kirkpatrick. "I probably would, but I always told the truth. I said those shoes were off the horse, and I never once said they'd been on the horse."

"He (Nashua) was a real bargain then and now," recalled Combs in a 1967 *Daily Racing Form* interview. "Nashua had more natural racing ability than any horse I ever saw. But he was a clown and a joker. You can count the fingers on one hand the times he leveled and did his very best. He would go a mile and a quarter, win by a head, and not be overly tired. Or he would take the lead and loaf, waiting for some horse to catch up again. Looking at his record though, Nashua usually got there."

Nashua's popularity continued on and off the racetrack as a favorite of visitors to Spendthrift.

Nashua with his groom Clem Brooks

"Last year more than seventy-thousand people had signed Nashua's guestbook," Combs recalled in a 1960 interview with the *Saturday Evening Post*. "Early last June there were 3,700 people at a convention in Lexington, and when I tried to get in here the cop said 'you can't come in.' All the lanes were crowded with buses, and I didn't want to embarrass him, so I drove around and came in by barn 14. When I got in, here came the voice of my groom, Clem Brooks, talking about Nashua over loud speakers. There were people everywhere. Clem was a character, he always gave the tourists a horse shoe that belonged to Nashua. If Nashua had worn that many shoes, he would have been a centipede."

Although Combs wasn't able to purchase Swaps, the various twists and turns of the great horse's life eventually led him to stand alongside his old rival Nashua at Spendthrift Farm.

In 1956, Swaps returned in a blaze of glory to set seven new track, world, or stakes records in an amazing display chronicled by journalist Morton Cathro who wrote, "The ease with which he set those world records, going to the front and just saying goodbye, just more or less humbling his opponents – all of this despite a recurring foot problem that never really went away entirely – look at the charts – in many of his races where he set world records he was eased up. He was just so, so spectacular, and so dominating." Swaps was inducted into the Hall of Fame in 1966.

In October 1956, while training for the Washington D.C. International at Laurel Park in Maryland, Swaps fractured his left hind cannon bone in two places. If that wasn't traumatic enough, a week later, he whacked his leg in the stall, shattered the cast, and extended the fracture into the pastern. Swaps' life hung in the balance. Trainer Fitzsimmons sent Mesh Tenney a special sling from Belmont Park, and Swaps literally hung from the barn rafters unable to bear weight on the injured leg. The great horse had to be lowered and raised for circulatory reasons every 45 minutes, and was monitored around the clock by the watchful eye of Tenney. Swaps dealt with his injury with intelligence and patience. In November 1956 the cast was removed, and preparations were made to send Swaps off to stud.

Swaps stood his first season in California at Rex Ellsworth's farm. The following year, the son of Your Host was moved to John Galbreath's

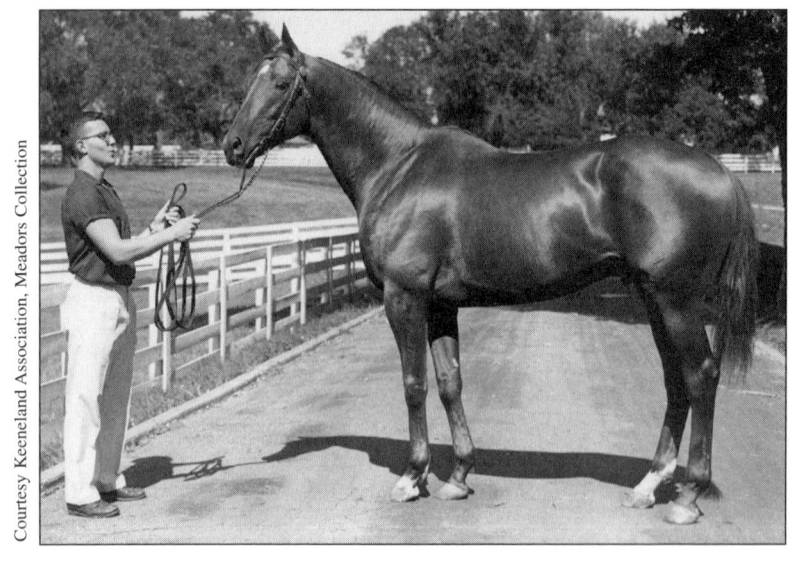

Courtesy Keeneland Association, Meadors Collection

Swaps stood at Spendthrift Farm during his last five years at stud.

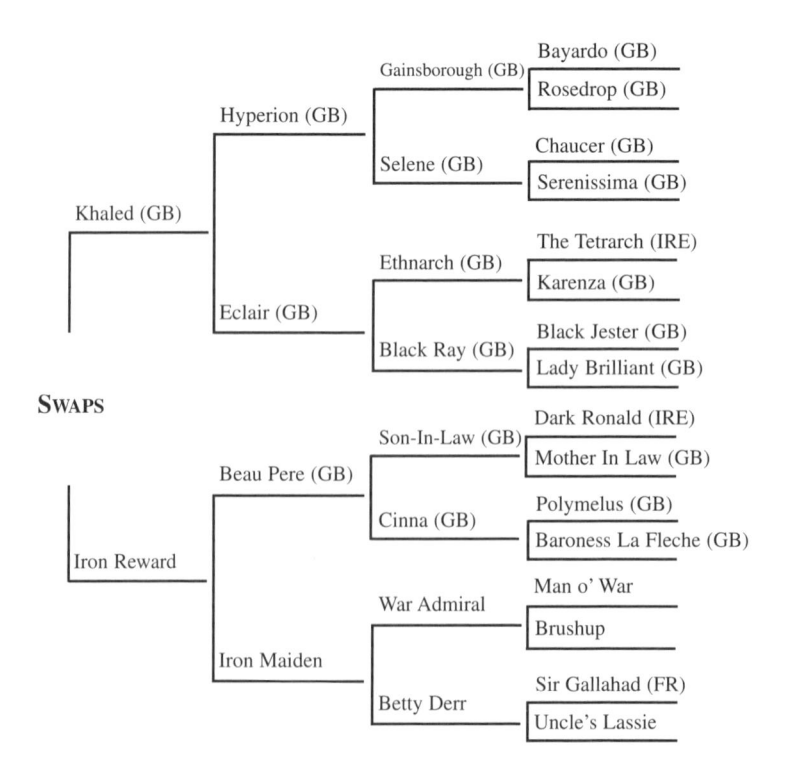

SWAPS

- Khaled (GB)
  - Hyperion (GB)
    - Gainsborough (GB)
      - Bayardo (GB)
      - Rosedrop (GB)
    - Selene (GB)
      - Chaucer (GB)
      - Serenissima (GB)
  - Eclair (GB)
    - Ethnarch (GB)
      - The Tetrarch (IRE)
      - Karenza (GB)
    - Black Ray (GB)
      - Black Jester (GB)
      - Lady Brilliant (GB)
- Iron Reward
  - Beau Pere (GB)
    - Son-In-Law (GB)
      - Dark Ronald (IRE)
      - Mother In Law (GB)
    - Cinna (GB)
      - Polymelus (GB)
      - Baroness La Fleche (GB)
  - Iron Maiden
    - War Admiral
      - Man o' War
      - Brushup
    - Betty Derr
      - Sir Gallahad (FR)
      - Uncle's Lassie

58

Darby Dan Farm in Lexington. Combs finally got to stand Swaps during his last five years at stud. The great horse was put down in November 1972 at the age of 20.

Combs put together many successful stallion syndications worth well over $1 million including Spendthrift Farm-bred Raise a Native ($2,625,000) and Majestic Prince ($1.8 million), Never Bend ($1,225,000), Creme Dela Creme ($1.2 million), and Exclusive Native ($1,920,000) – all highly significant and industry-altering prices for the times.

The success in breeding horses, according to Combs, was translating stallions into numbers. Spendthrift Farm was well known for standing over 30 stallions at one time.

"No one knows where a good stud will come from," Combs reflected. "That's why I've always wanted as many as I could get."

The unique U-shaped stallion barn at Spendthrift was home to over 160 stallions over the years.

NASHUA SYNDICATE AGREEMENT

THIS AGREEMENT, made as of December 15, 1955, between the several persons whose names and addresses are set out in the Schedule hereto attached as the original Subscribers, and being referred to collectively as "the Shareholders,"

WITNESSETH:

WHEREAS, Leslie Combs II, Spendthrift Farm, Ironworks Pike, Lexington, Kentucky, has purchased the thoroughbred horse NASHUA (B.c., 1952), by *NASRULLAH-SEGULA, by JOHNSTOWN from the Estate of William Woodward, Jr. and has formed a Syndicate to acquire the ownership thereof upon the following terms and conditions:

1. The ownership of NASHUA shall be divided into thirty-two (32) shares, and the purchasers of said thirty-two (32) shares have paid the total purchase price of One Million, Two Hundred and Fifty-One Thousand, Two Hundred Dollars, ($1,251,200.00), or the sum of Thirty-Nine Thousand, One Hundred Dollars ($39,100.00) per share.

2. Each of the thirty-two (32) shares shall be on an equal basis with the others and shall be indivisible, and only a full share shall have any of the rights hereunder; provided, however, that there is expressly reserved, and the within sale is made subject to one (1) free nomination to NASHUA each year during his life for each of the following named persons, their heirs and assigns: John W. Hanes, 460 Park Avenue, New York City, C. J. Devine, 48 Wall Street, New York City, and Leslie Combs II, Spendthrift Farm, Lexington, KY.

3. NASHUA shall be returned to training as soon as practicable and shall race under the personal management and supervision of a Committee consisting of John W. Hanes, C. J. Devine, and Leslie Combs II, as agents for the shareholders. The Committee shall have full charge of and complete control over the future racing career of

NASHUA, including but not limited to (a) the employment of a trainer, (b) the selection of tracks at which he will be trained and raced, (c) the races to which he will be nominated and in which he will be actually started, (d) the selection and employment of a jockey or jockeys, (e) the name and colors under which he will be raced, and (f) how long NASHUA shall race and when he shall be retired from racing, and the actions, decisions and judgments of the Committee with respect to any and all of the foregoing matters shall be final, conclusive and binding upon all of the Shareholders and shall not give rise to any liability upon the Committee or the individual members thereof so long as they act in good faith.

All expenses incurred by the Committee in training and racing NASHUA shall be paid by the Shareholders in proportion to the number of shares owned by each of them, and the earnings of NASHUA shall likewise be divided amongst the Shareholders proportionately. The Committee shall furnish each Shareholder periodically with a statement showing the expenses and earnings.

The Committee is authorized to execute such leases or other instruments as may be required under the rules of The Jockey Club and/or the various Racing Commissions and other governmental bodies having jurisdiction of the premises to qualify NASHUA to race.

If a member of the Committee should die, resign or be unable to serve for any reason, then the remaining members of the Committee shall select his successor from amongst the Shareholders.

4. Upon retirement to the stud, NASHUA shall stand and shall be kept and maintained at Spendthrift Farm, Ironworks Pike, in Fayette County, Kentucky, under the sole personal management and supervision of Leslie Combs II, and he shall be entitled to charge and receive the prevailing rates for stallion keep. Leslie Combs II shall have complete charge of advertising the stallion and shall have the authority to select a veterinarian. Owners of shares shall pay all charges, costs and expenses incurred in connection with said stallion in the proportion that their respective shares bear to the whole number of shares.

5. Each Shareholder in each breeding season shall be entitled to one (1) free nomination to said stallion for each share owned by him, subject to the payment of his share of the Syndicate expenses and the provisions of Paragraph 6; provided, however, that in NASHUA'S first full season in the stud he shall be limited to a book of twenty-five (25) mares, and the owners of the thirty-two (32) shares and the holders of the three (3) free nominations each year (as provided in Paragraph 2) who collectively are entitled to the twenty-five (25) nominations shall be determined by lot at a drawing to be held at such time and place as the aforesaid Committee may determine, and notice of which shall be sent by registered mail or by telegram to each Shareholder at least five (5) days prior thereto. Each share and each free nomination shall be regarded as if it were the subject of separate ownership and shall be on an equal basis, the one with the other.

Thereafter, if the veterinarian attending said stallion and the Syndicate Manager, Leslie Combs II, shall certify that in their opinion NASHUA'S book may be increased without injury to him, then additional yearly nominations may be sold by the Syndicate Manager at the regular stud fee and the yearly proceeds thereof shall be divided among the Shareholders in proportion to the number of shares owned by each.

Each mare bred to NASHUA must be in sound breeding condition and free from infection or disease, and no mare shall be covered more than six (6) times in any breeding season.

6. If Leslie Combs II, with the advice and approval of the veterinarian shall determine that NASHUA shall be bred to less than thirty-five (35) mares in any stud season, then the Shareholders and those persons holding the three (3) free nominations in each year (as provided in Paragraph 2 herein) who collectively shall be entitled to such reduced number of nominations shall be determined by lot, and any Shareholder or holder of said free nominations who has suffered by reason of the drawing of lots in any season shall not be submitted to the risk of drawing in any subsequent season unless and until all other Shareholders and holders of said free nominations, have suffered as the result thereof; and for the purpose of this clause each share and

free nomination shall be regarded as if it were the subject of separate ownership and shall be on an equal basis, the one with the other. Notice of the decision to reduce NASHUA'S book to less than thirty-five (35) nominations and of the time and place of the drawing shall be sent by the Syndicate Manager to each Shareholder and holder of a free nomination by registered mail or by telegram at least five (5) days prior to said drawing.

7. Leslie Combs II shall employ the usual care customarily employed in Fayette County, Kentucky, in the management of NASHUA, but shall not be responsible for any injury, disease or death of said stallion, nor for any injury, disease or death of any mare resulting from breeding or attempted breeding to said stallion.

8. Leslie Combs II shall have and is hereby granted the right and option to purchase any share or shares which any owner desires to sell, and such owner shall first offer the same to Leslie Combs II with the price requested for the same. If Leslie Combs II is unwilling to pay the price requested by the owner, then such owner may secure a written offer elsewhere for such share or shares, and if the owner is willing to accept such written offer he shall present the same to Leslie Combs II, who shall have the right to purchase, within forty-eight hours thereafter, such share or shares for the price so offered in writing and which the owner was willing to accept. In the event Leslie Combs II fails to purchase such share or shares within the time specified, then such owner may accept such written offer. This option shall apply in the same manner and under the same conditions to such share or shares in the new ownership. This option shall apply to and have priority over any hypothecation, distraint or other alienation of said share or shares or any interest therein, and any and all transfers of any share or shares are expressly subject to said option.

9. All notices required hereunder shall be effective and binding if sent by prepaid registered mail, telegram, cable, or delivered in person to the address of the respective Shareholders set out in the Schedule attached or such address as shall hereafter be designated in writing to the Syndicate Manager.

10. The Shareholders accept delivery of NASHUA without examination as to his fertility and breeding soundness, as no veterinary examination with reference thereto has been made or will be made prior to his retirement from racing.

11. The undersigned hereby subscribes for _____ shares in the Syndicate for the total sum of $_____, payable in cash upon the execution of this Agreement, and in consideration thereof Leslie Combs II has sold and conveyed _____ shares to undersigned, subject to all of the terms and conditions herein.

This Agreement may be executed in several counterparts, and when executed by the Shareholders the several counterparts shall constitute the agreement between the parties as if all signatures were appended to one original instrument.

WITNESS the hand of the undersigned as of the day and date first above written.

_____
Name

_____
Address

_____
Approved:

_____
Syndicate Manager

CHAPTER SIX

MYRTLEWOOD

Combs admitted on more than one occasion that the majority of his Thoroughbred knowledge had been gained from his Uncle Brownell Combs, who provided him with a foundation for Spendthrift's breeding and sales success in the great broodmare Myrtlewood.

Brownell purchased Myrtlewood's dam, Frizeur, from John E. Madden, the owner of Hamburg Place on Winchester Road in Lexington. Frizeur was a daughter of the Kentucky-bred Two Thousand Guineas winner Sweeper II and the great taproot mare Frizette, sired by Madden's iron horse and stayer Hamburg.

Foaled in 1932, Myrtlewood was born when Frizeur was 16 years old. The older mare's produce record was solid if not exemplary, as she had produced three prior stakes winners in Crowning Glory, Pairbypair, and Black Curl.

Myrtlewood's sire was the classy Blue Larkspur, bred by Colonel E.R. Bradley's Idle Hour Stock Farm near Lexington. Blue Larkspur, a member of the speedy Domino sire line, was the champion three-year-old of 1929, and also won the Belmont Stakes that year. He sired 44 stakes winners during his career.

"Much of the breeding success of Spendthrift Farm can be credited to Myrtlewood and her daughters," said Brownell Combs. "We had Myrtlewood daughters everywhere. Even if they couldn't run, you could guarantee that they would throw something that could. They were great broodmares, and the absolute essence of our breeding program. The Myrtlewood daughters were like gold; everybody wanted one."

Myrtlewood, winner of the 1936 Keen Handicap and Ashland Stakes, G. South up at Keeneland's opening meet.

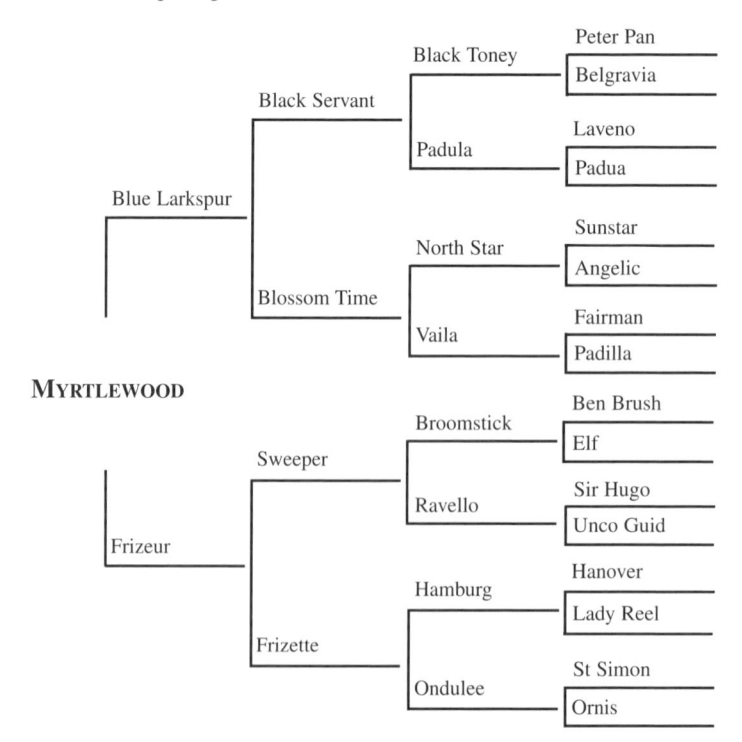

MYRTLEWOOD

```
                                              ┌── Peter Pan
                              ┌── Black Toney ┤
                              │               └── Belgravia
              ┌── Black Servant┤
              │               │               ┌── Laveno
              │               └── Padula ─────┤
              │                               └── Padua
Blue Larkspur ┤
              │                               ┌── Sunstar
              │               ┌── North Star ─┤
              │               │               └── Angelic
              └── Blossom Time┤
                              │               ┌── Fairman
                              └── Vaila ──────┤
                                              └── Padilla

                                              ┌── Ben Brush
                              ┌── Broomstick ─┤
                              │               └── Elf
              ┌── Sweeper ────┤
              │               │               ┌── Sir Hugo
              │               └── Ravello ────┤
              │                               └── Unco Guid
Frizeur ──────┤
              │                               ┌── Hanover
              │               ┌── Hamburg ────┤
              │               │               └── Lady Reel
              └── Frizette ───┤
                              │               ┌── St Simon
                              └── Ondulee ────┤
                                              └── Ornis
```

66

The physical description of Myrtlewood conjures a vision of a beautifully balanced athlete, as John Hervey so eloquently stated in *American Racehorses of 1936*, "She stands full sixteen hands tall, has a bloodlike, hawky head and a long, elegant neck." She possessed a body that was "robust and powerful, but of fine lines and proportions, and legs of good bone. In appearance she was regal upon the course, having the high carriage and queenly ways, though her deportment was at all times quiet and controlled."

Brownell handed the education of Myrtlewood over to trainer Ray Kindred, who fostered the filly's talents with care during her two-year-old season. As a juvenile, Myrtlewood made only four starts, closing the season with two wins, a second, and a third in the 1934 Kentucky Jockey Club Stakes at Churchill Downs.

In 1935, the game bay filly returned to the racetrack mature and freshened. After winning a seven-furlong allowance race at Arlington Park in her debut, Myrtlewood sailed to a three-length win and a new American record for six furlongs in 1:09 2/5 in an allowance race also at Arlington. Energizing fans with her front-running brilliance, Myrtlewood scored a 1 1/2-length tally over John F. Clark's speedy gelding Clang in the one mile F.S. Peabody Memorial Handicap. The race sparked a hot sprinting rivalry between the two horses that would continue throughout the season.

Clang was always within striking distance of Myrtlewood, as she stormed down the straight to snatch the laurels away from her gutsy rival. As a result of Clang's "near misses" against the daughter of Blue Larkspur, Clark called for the first of two match races against Myrtlewood in order to prove that it was just a matter of timing.

In their initial match at Hawthorne Racecourse on September 25, Myrtlewood's tenacity proved best by a nose after a hard driving duel down the stretch with Clang nearly matching her stride-for-stride, covering six furlongs in 1:10 4/5 – just a tick off her original track record. In their second test at Cincinnati on October 12, it took all of Clang's reserves to hold off the filly's blazing kick as he dug in to win by a nose in 1:09 1/5, breaking Myrtlewood's previous record.

It was the final shot of glory for Clang, who would never sail past Myrtlewood on the racetrack again. As a four-year-old, the Blue Larkspur filly went on to win divisional honors as champion sprinter of 1936 with eight wins from 10 starts, while setting a new track record of 1:10 3/5 in the Cadillac Handicap at Detroit that year. She closed her career with three-length win over Miss Merriment in a match race at the newly-crowned Keeneland racecourse. Overall, Myrtlewood won 15 of 22 starts, for earnings of $40,620. During her career, the durable runner held the American record for fillies and mares at six furlongs and a mile, and managed to set track records at five Midwestern racetracks. Myrtlewood was inducted into the Racing Hall of Fame in 1979.

After being retired to the pastures of Spendthrift Farm, Myrtlewood was bred to C.V. Whitney's great handicapper Equipoise, fondly known to the racing public as the "Chocolate Soldier." The resulting foal of 1938 was Crepe Myrtle, who failed to prove her merit on the racetrack with only one win from four starts, and earnings of $450.

Crepe Myrtle's success in the breeding shed far outweighed her lack of talent on the racetrack. In 1946, Crepe Myrtle produced Myrtle Charm, sired by Alsab, bred under the partnership of Leslie Combs II and Brownell Combs.

Myrtle Charm was purchased as a yearling for $27,000 by Lestor Manor Stable, who bought her as agent for cosmetics magnate Elizabeth Arden Graham, eventual owner of Maine Chance Farm in Lexington.

In her first start on August 9 at Washington, Myrtle Charm dusted the competition by eight lengths in a six-furlong maiden special. She returned to Saratoga on August 17 to win the six-furlong Spinaway Stakes by 12 lengths. Scintillating victories in the Matron Stakes and Modesty Handicap followed, and Myrtle Charm was named the champion two-year-old of 1948.

Several years later the daughter of Myrtle Charm named Fair Charmer became the dam of My Charmer, who produced 1977 Triple Crown winner Seattle Slew, the sire of 109 stakes winners. Seattle Slew, well known for his prancing "war dance" to the post, and his tough and tenacious running style, became the only undefeated Triple Crown winner in the history of the series. He died at Hill 'n Dale Farm from complications related to a degenerative spinal cord disease at the age of 28 in May 2002.

During her long and substantial career as a broodmare, Myrtle Charm also produced Frizette and Alcibiades Stakes winner Myrtle's Jet, by Jet Pilot, another Maine Chance acquisition.

Also descended from Crepe Myrtle is the stakes winner Masked Lady, who produced the stakes winner Who's To Know, the dam of graded stakes winner Angel Island. Angel Island, a grand producer in her own right, became the dam of international stakes winner and sire Sharrood, and stakes winners Island Escape (by Slew o' Gold, by Seattle Slew), and Our Reverie.

The first daughter of Myrtlewood became the direct tail female ancestor of a Triple Crown winner who evolved into one of the greatest Thoroughbred stallions in the last 20 years of the 20th Century. Her second daughter, Miss Dogwood, became the third dam of breed shaper Mr. Prospector, the sire of 165 stakes winners and a multitude of influential sires.

Miss Dogwood, a foal of 1939 sired by Bull Dog, continued to weave the fabric of fame for Spendthrift with a victory in the 1942 Kentucky Oaks and Phoenix Handicap. She also won two additional stakes, and placed in four others, retiring with 14 wins in 21 starts, for earnings of $31,712.

The produce record of Miss Dogwood was as equally impressive as her race record. Her stakes winners included Bernwood, Bella Figura, and Sequence. She also became the grandam of stakes winners Tumiga, Gold Digger (out of Sequence, by Count Fleet), Dedimoud, Noorsaga, Alert Princess, Peninsula Princess, Hermod, and Carrier X. However it was Gold Digger, two-time winner of the Gallorette Stakes and runner-up in the 1965 Kentucky Oaks, who would produce the most lasting impact of the Myrtlewood line through her son Mr. Prospector.

Gold Digger, a daughter of Nashua, kept the family tradition in line and produced three stakes winners in Gold Standard, Lillian Russell, and Mr. Prospector, sired by Spendthrift's new sire sensation, Raise a Native.

Mr. Prospector, consigned to the 1971 Keeneland July yearling sale, attracted a great deal of interested parties including the astute eye of trainer Warren A. "Jimmy" Croll, who was looking for a racing and sire prospect for Florida farm owner A.I. "Butch" Savin. In the early 1970s, top quality stallion prospects normally made their way to Kentucky not Florida. Savin opted to purchase his own colt, race it, and eventually stand it at stud in his home state. Under the recommendation of Croll, Savin purchased Mr. Prospector from Spendthrift for a sale-topping $220,000. It was one of the biggest bargains of the century.

During the summer of 1972, Mr. Prospector was training like a tiger, and Croll was pleased with what he saw. However, under Croll's watchful eye, Mr. Prospector may have been saved from a potential breakdown, after the trainer took heed on recommendation from an exercise rider and had the two-year-old son of Raise a Native x-rayed for posterity. The x-rays revealed nothing more than a minor injury, but Croll took a step back and gave the colt time to mature.

Showing precocious early speed typical of the Myrtlewood line, Mr. Prospector raised eyebrows as he zipped through six furlongs in 1:07 4/5 over the winter of 1973 at Gulfstream Park. He had missed his entire two-year-old season due to the injury, and Savin was ready to see what the horse could do. That year, Mr. Prospector won the Gravesend and Whirlaway Handicaps, solidifying his reputation as a sprinter, and retired to stand in Florida.

It wasn't long before the first crop of "Mr. P's" were making headlines, and the stallion moved to Claiborne Farm in Paris, Kentucky, to stand at stud for the entirety of his career. It may have seemed to be an insult to stand Mr. Prospector at a rival farm, but it actually worked to Spendthrift's advantage in the sales ring and the breeding shed for Raise a Native's stud career.

Although Mr. Prospector and his get have long been categorized as sprinters, he is well known as being more than a one-dimensional sire. Some of his most notable progeny that have become sires includes Belmont Stakes winner and Horse of the Year Conquistador Cielo, Gulch, Forty Niner, Fappiano, Kentucky Derby winner Fusaichi Pegasus, Woodman, Gone West, and Miswaki. Included among his champion fillies are Ravinella, Queena, and Golden Attraction.

During his lifetime, Mr. Prospector led the American sire and broodmare sire list on two occasions. He died at the age of 29 at Claiborne Farm in 1999.

Myrtlewood's third foal was the unimpressive Sicklewood, by Sickle. He was an absolute disappointment with one start in his career and no wins to his credit. The third foal, Durazna, by Bull Lea, was a different story.

Durazna, speedy and talented, churned out six wins over fillies and colts in her juvenile season to capture divisional honors as the champion two-year-old filly of 1943. In her three-year-old season, she was capable of besting the likes of 1944 champion three-year-old filly Twilight Tear and 1945 champion filly Busher. During her career, Durazna galloped past co-champion juvenile colt Occupy to take the Breeders' Futurity and Prairie States Stakes, and also whipped the colts one more time in the Hawthorne Juvenile Stakes. She also won the Beverly and Sheridan Handicaps among her nine wins from 19 starts for earnings of $70,201.

As a broodmare, Durazna made her mark into the modern era as a broodmare worthy of the Myrtlewood line. Her daughter Manzana produced stakes winner Journalette, who was in turn the dam of Typecast, 1972 champion older mare. She also produced Querida, the second dam of 1969 juvenile filly champion Tudor Queen and Irish champion Highest Trump – the second dam of English champion and sire Bahri and champion and 1977 Breeders' Cup winner Ajina.

Myrtlewood died in 1950 after producing the War Admiral colt Civic Virtue. She produced 11 foals, two stakes winners, and five winners from eight starters. She is the ancestress of over 250 stakes winners, and has two prolific sire lines that descend from her through the tail-female line. The final resting place of Myrtlewood is in the rose garden in front of Spendthrift's main residence where the flowers continue to bloom in her memory.

Chapter Seven

IDUN

The leggy bay filly with the left white front pastern caught the attention of trainer Sherrill Ward at the 1956 Keeneland summer yearling sale. She was beautifully balanced with a sloping shoulder, good bone, and a well-set hind leg with deep hindquarters. The daughter of *Royal Charger out of the Bull Lea matron Tige O'Myheart, stood over a great deal of ground for her size. The filly overtracked by three hoof prints at the walk, and glided over the ground with the ease of a dancer. Ward assumed that her gallop stride would match her conformation, and was determined to purchase her.

Ward, the eventual Hall of Fame trainer of multiple champion and horse of the year Forego, had an eye for a horse. He purchased the classy filly from the Spendthrift Farm consignment for $63,000, a then-record price for a yearling filly at auction. The filly, bred by Leslie Combs and J.W. Hanes, was purchased by Mrs. Charles Ulrick Bay, the widow of the former United States Ambassador to Norway. Bay usually named her horses according to Scandinavian mythology, and crowned Idun after the Norwegian goddess of immortal youth.

As a juvenile, Idun was nothing short of brilliant. Under Ward's conditioning, the game filly was undefeated in eight starts, and closed the season with $220,955 in earnings. It was the largest sum ever won by a two-year-old filly at that time, breaking Top Flight's record of $219,000 that stood for 26 years.

Bay, who managed her deceased husband's Wall Street firm and also held a seat on the stock exchange, bided her time with Idun's talents. The filly made her initial bow on July 19 in a maiden special weight at

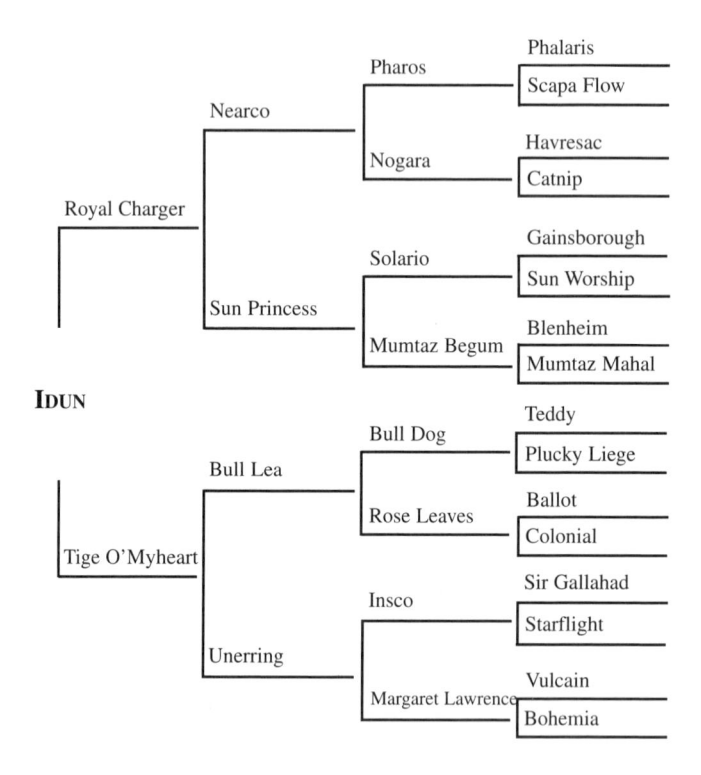

IDUN

- Royal Charger
  - Nearco
    - Pharos
      - Phalaris
      - Scapa Flow
    - Nogara
      - Havresac
      - Catnip
  - Sun Princess
    - Solario
      - Gainsborough
      - Sun Worship
    - Mumtaz Begum
      - Blenheim
      - Mumtaz Mahal
- Tige O'Myheart
  - Bull Lea
    - Bull Dog
      - Teddy
      - Plucky Liege
    - Rose Leaves
      - Ballot
      - Colonial
  - Unerring
    - Insco
      - Sir Gallahad
      - Starflight
    - Margaret Lawrence
      - Vulcain
      - Bohemia

Belmont Park. She finished second to Bridgework, but was placed first after the aforementioned was taken down for interference.

Idun's amazing string of victories began with a 3 1/2-length score in her second start, a 5 1/2-length allowance race at Saratoga Racecourse on August 15, 1957. Weaving through rivals, Idun shot to the lead and "drew out easily" to snatch her first victory under a game ride from jockey Eric Guerin.

Idun, champion 1957 2-year-old and 1958 3-year-old filly. Idun retired to the Spendthrift broodmare band with a record of 17 wins from 30 starts and $392,490 in earnings.

Although Idun showed a tendency toward laziness on the lead, it wasn't evident in her tenacious juvenile stakes wins. On September 21, Idun scored her first stakes victory with a three-length tally in the six-furlong Matron Stakes at Belmont Park. With eventual Hall of Fame jockey Bill Hartack in the irons, she notched a 3 1/2-length score in the 1 1/16-mile Gardenia Stakes at Gulfstream Park on October 19. Idun wrapped up divisional honors as the 1957 champion two-year-old filly with a 1 1/2-length win in the 1 1/16-mile Frizette Stakes and "scored as the rider pleased" according to the chart.

Idun had performed so brilliantly as a two-year-old that when it came time for the American Trainers Association to cast their votes for the best filly or mare of 1957 she received 72 votes, while Pucker Up received 41, Princess Turia gained four, and Bayou received two.

In her three-year-old debut on May 10, Idun won an allowance race at Garden State by eight lengths with the first quarter in a quick :22. After recovering from an intestinal upset following the six-furlong dash, she returned to Belmont Park two weeks later to finish fourth in an allowance race won by A Glitter. It was her poorest showing of the season. Ward attributed her poor performance to the fact that she had been shedding the caps from her teeth, which had caused excessive sensitivity in her mouth.

Ward's principal summer objective for Idun was the Coaching Club Oaks on June 21, but it never came to fruition. Ward was out of commission for a month with ruptured blood vessels in his leg after being kicked by a loose horse the day after Idun's first loss. Like her trainer, Idun remained idle for a month. The Acorn and Coaching Club Oaks took place while Ward was recovering.

Following Ward's return, Idun made her next start in typical fashion as she dashed to an easy three-length score in 1:11 in an allowance race at Belmont Park on June 27.

Idun made her three-year-old stakes debut in the 1 1/16-mile Mother Goose Stakes at Belmont on July 5. With Hartack in the irons, Idun grabbed the lead from the speedy Lea Moon after five furlongs, and zipped through six furlongs in 1:09 4/5 – only a fifth of a second off the track record. Cruising along with ease, Idun scored a three-length tally in 1:43 3/5 over Lopar, with Lea Moon in third, and Acorn Stakes winner Big Effort in fourth.

Idun once again faced off with her old rival C.C.A. Oaks winner A Glitter in the Delaware Oaks at Delaware Park on July 12. In spite of Hartack's efforts to keep the filly on the pace throughout the slop, Idun weakened in the stretch and finished second more than two lengths behind Big Effort.

Following her loss in the Delaware Oaks, Ward came to the conclusion that Idun needed more time between races. He bypassed Saratoga, with an eye on an allowance race at Belmont Park on September 5. Idun romped to an easy four-length score, running the mile in a game 1:36 2/5.

The allowance victory was the perfect prep for the 1 1/16-mile Gazelle Handicap at Belmont on September 15. Highweighted at 124 pounds, Idun increased her long lead with ease and outkicked rivals to post a 4 1/2-length victory. Munch, passing tiring rivals, finished second with Tempted in third, and A Glitter trailing in fourth.

Idun's victory in the Gazelle solidified divisional honors as the champion three-year-old filly of 1958, as she had consistently beaten the best of her sex. However, in her final three starts of the season, she ran well but not true to form. In her last start, she ran against the colts in the Roamer Handicap at Jamaica on November 8, and finished a game third behind Warhead.

Josephine Bay had remarried by the beginning of Idun's four-year-old season, and the filly raced under the name of Josephine Paul. Consistent and plucky, Idun captured four stakes victories in the Columbia, Colonial, Liberty Belle, and Maskette Handicaps. She retired with 17 wins from 30 starts, and $392,490 in earnings. Idun was ridden to all her stakes wins except one by champion jockey Hartack, who established a record-setting 43 stakes victories in 1957 among his many accomplishments.

Great expectations were attached to Idun as a broodmare, but her career in the breeding shed was unfortunate. Her first foal was a brown filly by Swaps named Bless Swaps, who managed to win one race from four starts. The second foal, a filly named Verana by Summer Tan, churned out one win from nine starts.

For the next five years, Idun's chances at motherhood were thwarted by repeated abortions, a barren year, and the birth of a dead foal. In 1969, she produced Beaverstone, a bay colt by Chateaugay, who made it to the races but never won. The Graustark filly Monochrome was foaled in 1971, and also never won a race.

Ben Adhem, a colt by champion and leading sire *Ribot, was foaled in 1972, and proved the best of Idun's offspring. Over four seasons, Ben Adhem won two stakes races and placed in seven others. He won nine of 47 starts, including the 1976 Independence Day and British Columbia Handicaps at Longacres.

Two of Idun's last three foals were winners; Lord Ligonier, by Graustark, and his full brother McCutcheon. Her last foal was North Bay, a colt by Good Counsel, foaled in 1979. Overall she produced nine foals, five winners, and eight starters.

In spite of her mediocre career as a broodmare, Idun carved out a niche in racing history as an amazingly consistent and sound racehorse with two championship titles to her credit.

CHAPTER EIGHT

GALLANT MAN

Gallant Man had the luck, or lack thereof, of being born in 1954 in the same crop as Bold Ruler and Round Table, whose domination of the three-year-old classics overshadowed his sheer brilliance. Gallant Man remains one of the most talented and courageous Thoroughbreds to grace the American turf without ever winning a championship title.

The small, well-made bay son of Migoli, out of Majideh, by Mahmoud, with the feathered star on his forehead was one of nine yearlings offered for sale in a package deal by his breeder, the Aga Kahn, and his son Aly. The group was purchased in Ireland by bloodstock agent Humphrey Finney and veterinarian Dr. D.L. Proctor on behalf of Midland, Texas, oil millionaire Robert Lowe for $220,000.

The colt, soon to be named Gallant Man, was not the most favored of the yearlings. The most highly-regarded yearling in the group was a colt named Prince Nero, who just happened to finish last in Gallant Man's Belmont Stakes win. Gallant Man was diminutive, although correct, and did not stand out among his strapping, growthy stablemates. As is often the case with horses, size had nothing to do with his ability and raw courage.

As a three-year-old, the inauspicious youngster grew to 15.1 hands of pure balance and power, with a compact build and an intelligent and regal bearing that belied his classic pedigree.

Gallant Man was sired by the Prix de l'Arc de Triomphe winner Migoli. His dam, Majideh, hailed from the line of Qurrat-Al-Ain, one of the Aga Kahn's most coveted broodmares, who had also won the Coronation and Queen Mary Stakes. Majideh, winner of the Irish Oaks and One Thousand Guineas, was sired by the brilliant Mahmoud. She also produced his half sister Masaka, another classic winner, who won the Irish and English Oaks. Gallant Man, inbred to Mahmoud, would reveal the signature classic speed that the line came to define.

Gallant Man never ran in a stakes race as a two-year-old. He won his third start at Hollywood Park at longshot odds of 50-to-1, and was sent east to trainer John Nerud for conditioning. Under Nerud's watchful eye, Gallant Man bloomed. He closed his two-year-old season with four wins from seven starts, and earnings of $7,075.

In his first start as a three-year-old, Gallant Man made the transition from a who's that to a who's who. The plucky bay set a new track record of 1:09 2/5 for six furlongs with a six-length win in an allowance race at Tropical Park on January 3, 1957. Gallant Man returned to post a half-length win in the six-furlong Hibiscus Stakes in a quick 1:10 on January 19 at Hialeah Park, prior to facing the swift Bold Ruler for their first meeting in the Bahamas Stakes on January 30.

Bold Ruler came into the Bahamas Stakes after a loss to Ambehaving in the Remsen Stakes. The staunch Nasrullah colt had been blocked, unable to find an opening, as Ambehaving ran off with the spoils. Game for a win, Bold Ruler scored an easy 4 1/2-length victory, while Gallant Man attempted a mild rally to finish fourth. In their next meeting, Gallant Man's tenacity shone through as he matched Bold Ruler stride-for-stride only to lose by a nose in the Wood Memorial Stakes in a new track record time of 1:48 4/5 for nine furlongs.

The Kentucky Derby would have belonged to Gallant Man instead of Iron Liege had it not been for jockey Bill Shoemaker's misjudgment of the finish line. The blunder goes down as one of the worst in racing history. Shoemaker stood up in the irons early, thinking that the race was over after passing the pagoda located in the infield. He instantly realized his mistake, and attempted to urge Gallant Man forward. However, it was too late, and the lapse in judgement allowed Bill Hartack aboard Iron Liege to win the race by a nose. There is no dispute as to who the winner would have been had Shoemaker not made the riding error.

At a dinner the night prior to the Kentucky Derby, Gallant Man's owner Ralph Lowe gave an account of a dream that he had envisioning

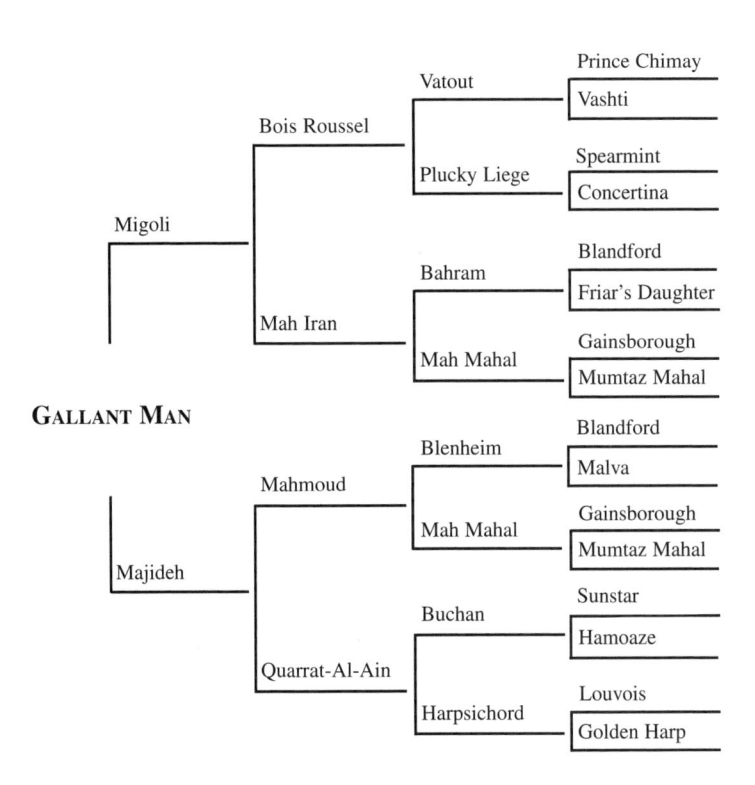

GALLANT MAN

- Migoli
  - Bois Roussel
    - Vatout
      - Prince Chimay
      - Vashti
    - Plucky Liege
      - Spearmint
      - Concertina
  - Mah Iran
    - Bahram
      - Blandford
      - Friar's Daughter
    - Mah Mahal
      - Gainsborough
      - Mumtaz Mahal
- Majideh
  - Mahmoud
    - Blenheim
      - Blandford
      - Malva
    - Mah Mahal
      - Gainsborough
      - Mumtaz Mahal
  - Quarrat-Al-Ain
    - Buchan
      - Sunstar
      - Hamoaze
    - Harpsichord
      - Louvois
      - Golden Harp

Shoemaker standing up in the irons prior to the finish of the race. Shoemaker, scoffed at the notion, stating "Well Ralph, now that we've heard about it, you don't have to worry." Lowe readily forgave Shoemaker for his mistake.

Nerud believed that Gallant Man liked a little more time between his races, and opted to skip the Preakness. The Peter Pan Handicap at Churchill Downs on June 1 provided him with the necessary preparation leading up to the Belmont Stakes. Gallant Man cruised past Iron Liege to win the 1 1/8-mile Peter Pan by 2 1/2 lengths. The victory set the stage for an exciting Belmont, as Gallant Man made his way to Belmont Park to face Preakness Stakes winner Bold Ruler with credentials as one of the finest stayers in the nation.

Gallant Man entered the Belmont Stakes alongside his stablemate and pacemaker Bold Nero, who prompted favorite Bold Ruler to zip through six furlongs in 1:10 2/5. Gallant Man, galloping along in fourth, was biding his time to strike.

Gallant Man, winner of the 1957 Belmont Stakes, with Bill Shoemaker Up and owner Ralph Lowe.

82

Lengthening his stride leaving the half-mile pole, Gallant Man hustled past rivals and gained the lead entering the stretch. Pulsating with speed in reserve, Gallant Man accelerated down the stretch to post an eight-length victory in the Belmont in a new American record of 2:26 3/5 for the 1 1/2 miles. Inside Tract finished a well-beaten second, with a tiring Bold Ruler struggling along four lengths back in third.

For the remainder of the 1957 season, Gallant Man added five additional victories to his resume, including wins in the Travers Stakes, Nassau County Handicap, and Jockey Club Gold Cup. He closed the season with a second-place finish to his old rival Bold Ruler in the Trenton Handicap, beaten by 2 1/4 lengths.

Gallant Man's four-year-old campaign in the handicap division was brief although brilliant. Bold Ruler, who had been sidelined with an ankle filling, won his first start of the season in the six-furlong Toboggan Handicap in a speedy 1:09 on May 17. In his first start of the season, Gallant Man hooked up with his old rival Bold Ruler. The game little bay closed well to finish third behind the champion son of Nasrullah in the Carter Handicap at Belmont Park on May 30.

The tables were turned in the Metropolitan Handicap on June 14 as Gallant Man drew clear under a game ride from Shoemaker to win by two lengths over Bold Ruler. With that victory under his girth, Gallant Man headed west. Carrying topweight of 130 pounds, Gallant Man scored a two-length win in the 1 1/4-mile Hollywood Gold Cup at Hollywood Park on July 12. He returned to the California oval less than two weeks later to tally a four-length score in the Sunset Handicap on July 22.

In his final start, Gallant Man was assigned 132 pounds in the Sysonby Handicap at Belmont on September 6. He finished unplaced in the Sysonby, which was won by Cohoes. Ironically, it was Cohoes that scored in Bold Ruler's final start in the Brooklyn Handicap on July 18 that year.

Bold Ruler was bestowed with divisional honors as the champion sprinter of 1958, and Round Table received the handicap championship title. Gallant Man was the only member of the "big three" not to win a divisional title during his brilliant career.

Leslie Combs had admired the exploits of Gallant Man, and had considered making an offer on the colt after he won the 1957 Hibiscus Stakes. Gallant Man was retired following the Sysonby due to a reoccurring splint condition in his forelegs. Overall, he won 14 of 24 starts, with earnings of $510,355. Combs finally made an offer to Lowe, and purchased a three-quarter interest in the colt for $1 million, and promptly syndicated Gallant Man for $1,333,333 in 1958.

Gallant Man, his face peppered with grey hairs inherited from his great grandsire Mahmoud, lived to the ripe old age of 34. He was euthanized in 1988 due to the infirmities of old age, and buried on Spendthrift Farm. Prior to his death, Gallant Man sired 52 stakes winners including champions Gallant Bloom and Spicy Living. He became well known as a sire of outstanding broodmares. His daughters produced Genuine Risk, and champions Lord Avie and Guilty Conscience.

CHAPTER NINE

RAISE A NATIVE AND HIS LINE

Leslie Combs was a commercial breeder, first and foremost. His primary objective was to breed the "best to the best and hope for the best," and Raise a Native was no exception.

Combs bred the Case Ace mare Raise You to Native Dancer in 1960, hoping that his philosophy would hold true. What Combs could not have foreseen was the immeasurable impact that the resulting foal would have on the Thoroughbred breeding industry.

Native Dancer, 1952 and 1954 Horse of the Year, was a blazingly fast, temperamental son of Polynesian, out of Geisha, by Discovery, who preferred to run races on his own terms. Prior to his first start, trainer Bill Winfrey revealed to reporters that "the gray is the fastest horse that I've ever trained. He shows good times in workouts, but that's not what's impressive. It's the fact that the big gray does it without any effort. He actually seems to be holding himself back."

Undefeated going into the 1953 Kentucky Derby, Native Dancer, "the Gray Ghost," went off at 3-to-5, the shortest odds in the history of the classic race. His Derby defeat by a nose to longshot Dark Star was the result of a bad bumping match at the start and down the stretch, although jockey Eric Guerin was blamed for "bad handling" facing the traffic problems during the race. Native Dancer, true to his championship style, never lost again. He was retired after being injured over a sloppy track while turning in a stunning nine-length score in the Oneonta Handicap at Saratoga Racecourse while carrying 137 pounds.

When Raise You foaled the strapping chestnut colt in 1961, Combs admired his spunk and abundance of muscling observing "that he

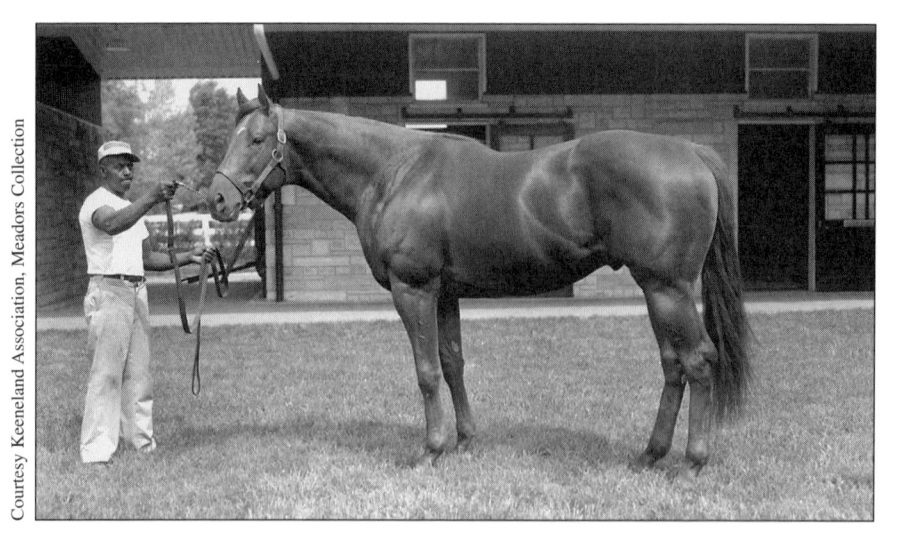

Raise a Native was syndicated by Leslie Combs for over $2.6 million.

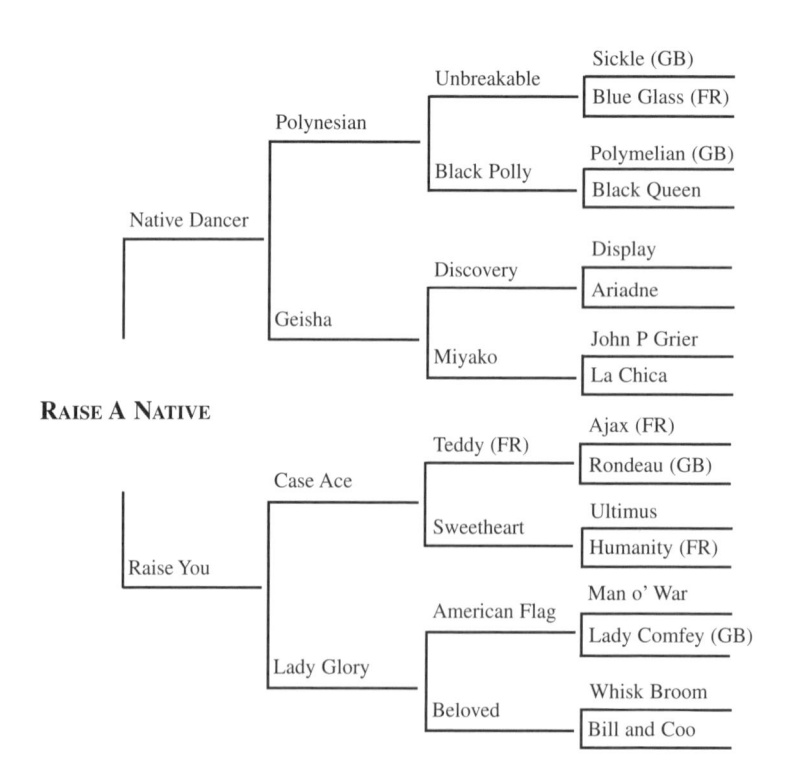

RAISE A NATIVE

- Native Dancer
  - Polynesian
    - Unbreakable
      - Sickle (GB)
      - Blue Glass (FR)
    - Black Polly
      - Polymelian (GB)
      - Black Queen
  - Geisha
    - Discovery
      - Display
      - Ariadne
    - Miyako
      - John P Grier
      - La Chica
- Raise You
  - Case Ace
    - Teddy (FR)
      - Ajax (FR)
      - Rondeau (GB)
    - Sweetheart
      - Ultimus
      - Humanity (FR)
  - Lady Glory
    - American Flag
      - Man o' War
      - Lady Comfey (GB)
    - Beloved
      - Whisk Broom
      - Bill and Coo

86

had the look of eagles right from the start" and "was up on his feet quicker than most." Raise a Native's stout musculature and catlike moves while playing foal games in the field were exemplary, but the true test would come on the racetrack.

Raise a Native was purchased for $39,000 by entrepreneur Louis Wolfson of Harbor View Farm at the 1962 Keeneland Sales. The stout colt looked like pure early speed, and was sent to Hall of Fame trainer Burley Parke for conditioning.

There is no better description of Raise a Native's lightning talent than the phrase coined by turf writer Red Smith who said that "the trees swayed" after watching the colt's workout one morning as he stretched out, pure muscle and motion, consuming the racetrack with every powerful stride.

Raise a Native was undefeated in four starts as a juvenile, and tied or equaled track records nearly every time he set his hooves on a racetrack. At Aqueduct, he zipped to a track record of :57 4/5 for five furlongs, and returned to equal the record by winning the 1963 Juvenile Stakes. He also set a track record for 5 1/2 furlongs in 1:02 3/5 with a tally in the Great American Stakes. The future looked bright, with an eye on the prestigious two-year-old races to follow in the summer and fall.

However, brilliance doesn't come without a price. Raise a Native inherited fragile ankles along with record-setting speed from Native Dancer, and the tied in tendons of his unsound stakes winning grandsire Case Ace. Raise a Native was forced into retirement after bowing a tendon. Although he never received divisional championship honors and missed the summer and fall championship races, he was named high weight two-year-old on the Experimental Free Handicap.

Raise a Native was retired to Harbor View Farm in 1963, and eventually relocated to Spendthrift in 1968 where he was syndicated by Combs for $2,625,000. Shares in Raise a Native sold like "water in the desert," with breeders eagerly awaiting their first foals by the latest Combs-created sire sensation.

"Now there's my idea of a good-looking stud prospect," Combs told the *Thoroughbred Record* in 1964. "That's Raise a Native, by Native

Dancer. He's got a masculine head, good shoulder, good flat bone, plenty of driving power, and above all is perfectly balanced. Looks like a four-year-old already. We've had over 100 applications to breed to him at $5,000 a season."

When the first crop of Raise a Native youngsters hit the ground running, a mere $5,000 stud fee became one of the biggest bargains of the century.

"The Raise a Natives were extremely good-looking and muscular," said Brownell Combs. "They looked like speed, like little quarterbacks. He stamped his foals regardless what kind of mare they were out of."

Exclusive Native was a member of Raise a Native's first crop out of Exclusive, by Shut Out. He inherited not only the rich chestnut coat of his sire but also the signature speed of the line. Exclusive Native won the Sanford Stakes as a two-year-old, and stretched out to win the Arlington Classic at three, but he had also inherited unsoundness.

Retired to Spendthrift Farm to stand alongside his sire, Exclusive Native was bred to many of the less expensive mares that resided at the farm. With the success of his son Our Native that all began to change. In 1973, the precocious Our Native won the Flamingo Stakes and Monmouth Invitational, and also secured a pair of third-place finishes in the Kentucky Derby and Preakness behind Secretariat and Sham.

The Crafty Admiral mare Won't Tell You was booked to Exclusive Native in 1974. Won't Tell You had been bred to the likes of Chieftain, Cornish Prince, Swaps, and even Raise a Native without producing a stakes winner or a high-class contender. So when she produced her seventh foal in 1975 there were no great expectations following his birth. However the choice of his name, Affirmed, might as well have been a premonition.

Wolfson's wife, Patrice, named Affirmed based on "the many important decisions, personal, business and otherwise that have been affirmed over the years," as chronicled in James B. Faulconer's *The Names They Give Them*. Wolfson said following a press conference for the 1977 Derby that his wife "likes 'Aff' on account of Affectionately, and we've had some good luck with these kinds of names...so far."

Won't Tell You did produce several high class runners following Affirmed's success. Stakes winners Love You Dear, Won't She Tell, and Grade 1-placed Silent Fox were all foaled in the last half of her broodmare career.

Also foaled in the same year was a handsome chestnut son of Raise a Native named Alydar, whose pedigree carried royal connections of the highest caliber. Bred by Calumet Farm, Alydar was out of the On-and-On mare Sweet Tooth, who had proven her merit as the dam of champion and three-time Grade 1 winner Our Mims.

According to Faulconer, Alydar got his name after Calumet owner Mrs. Gene Markey heard someone address the Aga Kahn as "Aly Dahling." She liked the sound of Alydar, and the stout colt had a name.

The roots of the Affirmed-Alydar debate began to grow well before the advent of the 1978 Triple Crown.

Alydar was highly touted by Calumet trainer John Veitch, who felt that a maiden special weight would not challenge the talented juvenile. Making his first start in the 1977 Youthful Stakes on June 15 at Belmont Park, Alydar finished a disappointing fifth while Affirmed cruised to win his second start by a neck. It did not take long for Alydar to find his form. In his second start, he won a maiden special at Belmont by 6 3/4 lengths with Believe It in second. He followed that victory with a 3 1/2-length tally over Affirmed in the Great American Stakes on July 27, where the Exclusive Native colt was deemed "no match" on that particular day.

Affirmed, trained by master horseman Lazaro Barrera, racked up four consecutive stakes victories following his defeat to Alydar in the Great American. He won the Juvenile Championship Stakes at Hollywood Park on July 23 by seven lengths, and earned a highly anticipated trip to Saratoga. Alydar galloped to victory in the Tremont and Sapling Stakes while Affirmed scampered to a 2 3/4-length tally over Tilt Up in the Sanford Stakes.

Alydar and Affirmed had defined the highest class of form for the 1977 juvenile championship. Now it was just a matter of time to determine which Raise a Native-line two-year-old would be honored as the divisional champion.

"The difference in ability between Alydar and Affirmed was not apparent," said Brownell. "Look at their margins of victory; they nearly always matched each other stride for stride to win by a head, a neck, a length. The greatest difference between the two was that Affirmed had Laz Barrera to train him. He was one of the last great horsemen."

Affirmed dashed to a half-length win over Alydar in the Hopeful Stakes at Saratoga, and put a nose in front to win the Futurity Stakes at Belmont. Alydar, unshakable, came back to collect a 1 1/4-length notch over that rival in the Champagne Stakes. At the closure of a grueling two-year-old season, Affirmed out-gunned Alydar down the stretch to win the Laurel Futurity by a neck and clinch divisional honors. Star de Naskra, a talented runner named champion sprinter in 1979, finished 10 lengths behind the duo.

With eight wins from 10 starts as a juvenile, and three Grade 1 wins to his credit, Affirmed was named the champion two-year-old in 1977. Alydar turned in five wins for the season, with two Grade 1 victories. He closed the season with a second-place finish to Believe It in the Remsen Stakes on November 26.

Hall of Fame trainer Woody Stephens, who conditioned Believe It, called the Affirmed and Alydar rivalry "the greatest act horse racing ever had. I hope it never ends."

The racing public had the Affirmed-Alydar debate firmly in place at the close of the 1977 racing season. The clash of the three-year-old titans en route to the Triple Crown was as highly anticipated as the boxing bouts between George Foreman and Muhammad Ali. At the end of the Triple Crown trail there would be no doubting the versatility of the Raise a Native sire line.

Undefeated in four starts leading up to the Kentucky Derby, Affirmed had scored a scintillating eight-length win in the Santa Anita Derby and a two-length victory in the Hollywood Gold Cup.

Alydar shared an equal amount of victories but three impressive Grade 1 wins, including the Flamingo Stakes, Florida Derby, and an astounding 13-length romp in the Bluegrass Stakes.

In the Derby, Alydar rated toward the back of the pack in ninth, and decisively threaded through the ranks approaching Affirmed, ridden by 18-year-old media darling Steve Cauthen, galloping along on the lead. Turning on the acceleration down the stretch, it was too late for a fast-closing Alydar, with Jorge Velasquez in the irons, to out-gun a fully extended Affirmed as he out-kicked that rival by 1 1/2 lengths.

Television and print media gnawed on the exploits of Affirmed and Alydar with the zest of hungry wolves. Never had there been such a rivalry in the racing world that inspired the masses to take sides. Would Affirmed take the Triple Crown, or would Alydar be the spoiler? The speculations flew and the headlines blazed.

Cauthen hustled Affirmed to an early lead in the Preakness Stakes, while Alydar shadowed the pace within striking distance in sixth. Moving through horses with tactical precision, Alydar closed with his signature kick but was unable to snatch the laurels from Affirmed as they battled down the stretch. Affirmed, relentless and unwilling to abdicate his hold on the lead, held on to win by a neck over Alydar's game effort.

The only thing that stood in front of Affirmed and a Triple Crown win was Alydar. The campaign had been long and difficult, and Affirmed was beginning to feel the effects. Cauthen continued to remain cool and collected under pressure, and told *Sports Illustrated* "I didn't think we'd have to fight it out for a mile, but with Affirmed and Alydar, it always seems to turn out that they fight for every inch."

In the Belmont, Affirmed jumped to the lead with Alydar poised to strike from third. Shortly after the half-mile, Alydar flanked his rival and matched him stride-for-stride from the three-quarter-pole. Gaining a brief lead, Alydar dug in but was refuted by Affirmed, pinning his ears and banging away down the stretch, as he held on to put a head in front in one of the most tenacious duels in racing history. The time for the 12-furlong Belmont was 2:26 4/5 – recorded as the third fastest time in the history of the race up to 1978.

Cauthen commented after the race that Affirmed "seemed to be tiring as we swung into the stretch, but then he saw Alydar right alongside, took a deep breath and switched leads, and seemed to race with fresh determination."

Affirmed's Triple Crown laurels were hard won, along with honors as the champion three-year-old of 1978. After a near two-month layup but a vastly short rest period, Affirmed returned to action to win the Jim Dandy Stakes at Saratoga. The remainder of a brilliant three-year-old season was plagued with mishap.

In their final meeting on the battleground, Affirmed and Alydar parted ways on a negative note. Jorge Velasquez claimed foul against Laffit Pincay, substituting in the irons for an injured Cauthen, after cutting off Alydar and causing him to check. Although Affirmed crossed the line first, he was disqualified and placed second to Alydar.

In the Marlboro Stakes two Triple Crown winners battled it out. Seattle Slew issued a three-length trouncing to Affirmed who was granted "no excuse" on the chart. Affirmed's saddle slipped in the Jockey Club Gold Cup during an all-out duel to the wire with Seattle Slew, and Exceller sailed past both warriors to post a nose victory. Affirmed faded 18 3/4 lengths back in fifth with tack trouble.

It was discovered that Alydar had broken a coffin bone during the Travers Stakes on August 19. He returned as a four-year-old in March to win an allowance race at Hialeah, but never truly returned to form. From six starts in 1979, Alydar posted one stakes win in the Nassau County Handicap, his second to last start.

After a third-place finish in the Suburban Handicap, Alydar was retired to Calumet Farm where he attracted the best mares in the industry. The ruggedly handsome son of Raise a Native nearly topped the American sire list on several occasions, and finally achieved that feat in 1990.

Included among Alydar's most famous offspring are 1988 Horse of the Year, two-time champion, and sire Alysheba – winner of the 1987 Kentucky Derby and Preakness Stakes; Calumet's sixth and final Horse of the Year, Criminal Type; 1989 Belmont Stakes winner, 1988 champion two-year-old, and sire Easy Goer; 1986 champion handicap horse and sire, Turkoman; 1982 champion filly Althea; undefeated juvenile stakes winner and sire, Saratoga Six; multiple graded stakes winner and producer

Miss Oceana; and 1991 Kentucky Derby winner and sire Strike the Gold. Alydar sustained multiple fractures to his hind leg in a barn accident, and was put down in the fall of 1990. The great stallion which never won an Eclipse award left behind a legacy of champions through his sons and daughters worldwide. Alydar was inducted into the Racing Hall of Fame in 1989.

Affirmed was named 1979 Horse of the Year after a brilliant four-year-old campaign. He churned out seven wins from nine starts that year, and retired after a 3/4-length win in the 1979 Jockey Club Gold Cup. He retired with 22 wins, five seconds, and a third from 29 starts, and then-record earnings of $2,393,818 as the first Thoroughbred to win over $2 million.

Trainer Laz Barrera once told *Sports Illustrated* that "Affirmed is greater than Secretariat, or any Triple Crown winner, because only Affirmed had to face Alydar."

Wolfson decided to retire the great champion to Spendthrift Farm, where he was syndicated for a then-record $14.4 million by Brownell Combs. Affirmed's success as a sire was not quite as spectacular as that of Alydar, but he shined brilliantly in his own right. Known for siring solid turf and dirt performers, Affirmed's daughter Flawlessly was named 1992 and 1993 champion grass mare. He also sired 1993 Canadian Triple Crown winner and sire Peteski. His daughters are highly sought after as broodmares. Affirmed sired over 80 stakes winners and nine champions in an enviable career.

Affirmed, inducted into the Racing Hall of Fame in 1980, was euthanized in 2001 after succumbing to laminitis. He is buried with the famous flamingo pink silks of Harbor View Farm at Jonabell Farm in Lexington, where he stood in later years.

Genuine Risk's pedigree was a combination of the best of Spendthrift. She was a daughter of Raise a Native's son Exclusive Native out of Gallant Man's daughter Virtuous. Bred by Spendthrift client Sally Humphrey and raced by Diana Firestone, Genuine Risk became the second filly to win the Kentucky Derby in 1980, following Regret in 1915 and preceding Winning Colors in 1988. In fact, she almost won the Triple Crown.

The elegantly feminine and blaze-faced Genuine Risk began her racing career in modest fashion. Trained by Leroy Jolley, she won her first start as a two-year-old by 1 3/4 lengths in a maiden special weight at Belmont Park on September 30, 1979, and returned to post a 7 1/4-length victory in a $15,000 allowance race at that same oval on October 18.

With a win under her girth, Genuine Risk made her next start in the Tempted Stakes on November 5 at Aqueduct. Gaining the lead early in the race, the Exclusive Native filly romped away to a smart three-length win over Street Ballet. She closed her juvenile season undefeated in four starts with a nose tally over eventual two-year-old champion filly Smart Angle in the Demoiselle Stakes.

The creation of Genuine Risk's three-year-old campaign was largely a byproduct of media hype based on the "battle of the sexes" and a preeminent feminist movement that was prevalent in the late 1970s and early 1980s. There was no disputing the fact that she was unbeaten against fillies, but was she good enough to race against boys? Only a test against the best colts of her generation would determine whether she could "have it all" as the outspoken feminists of the era loved to spout.

Genuine Risk made her first start against the colts in the Wood Memorial at Aqueduct on April 19, 1980. The tough filly was charted as giving it a "game try" but finished a plucky third to eventual sprint champion Plugged Nickel. It was hardly a performance worthy of a trip to Kentucky. Jolley was not keen about taking on the colts at Churchill Downs, but Bert and Diana Firestone had the final say. Genuine Risk would start in the Derby.

Genuine Risk, off at odds of 15-to-1, shadowed the pace from seventh in the early going with Jorge Vasquez in the irons. Sifting through the ranks, the filly surged to the lead entering the stretch, and held off a game closing drive from Rumbo and Jaklin Klugman to win by a length.

The media fed on the victory like starving hounds, and the battle of the sexes was in full swing.

Headlines screamed "You've Come A Long Way Baby" with a photo of Genuine Risk winning the Derby. The Preakness was only two weeks away, and fans were deeply divided. Could Genuine Risk become the fourth filly to win the Preakness? The only missing link in the Derby had been tough Santa Anita Derby winner Codex, trained by a then relatively unknown trainer named D. Wayne Lukas. The outcome of the 1980 Preakness would become one of the most controversial races of the decade.

Codex, with scrappy jockey Angel Cordero Jr. aboard, made a well-defined move to snatch the lead on the turn for home. Cordero, seeking every advantage, forced Genuine Risk to travel wide as she ranged up within striking distance. Codex sailed to a 4 3/4-length win, with Genuine Risk in second. The image of a defenseless filly being bullied down the stretch by an unruly colt did not set well with the media, the public, or the Firestones. After an appeal to the Maryland Racing Commission that led to a three-ring circus of a trial, the Firestones were required to let the results stand.

In the Belmont Stakes, Genuine Risk didn't have to worry about Codex...it was 50-to-1 longshot Temperance Hill who came surging down the lane. Digging in with tenacity, Genuine Risk tried with all her might to hold off the late charging son of Stop the Music as he powered to a two-length win. Genuine Risk held for second, while Preakness Stakes spoiler Codex faded to seventh. Following her gutsy performance in all three Triple Crown races and a victory in the Ruffian Handicap, Genuine Risk was honored as the 1980 champion three-year-old filly.

She returned to action as a four-year-old to compile two wins from three starts in allowance company. A knee injury forced Genuine Risk into retirement at the Firestone's Newstead Farm in Upperville, Virginia, in 1981. Genuine Risk was never off the board in 15 starts, with 10 wins, three seconds, and two thirds. She was inducted into the Hall of Fame in 1986.

Genuine Risk was bred to Secretariat in 1982, and sadly, the foal was a stillborn colt. Although scheduled to be bred to Nijinsky II in 1983, she was ultimately rebred to Secretariat and did not conceive. During the next 17 years, Genuine Risk only produced two live foals – Genuine Reward, by Rahy, in 1993 and Count Our Blessing, by Chief Honcho, in 1996. Neither of her offspring ever made it to the races. Count Our Blessing became a gelding, and Genuine Reward stands at stud in Wyoming.

Currently the oldest living Kentucky Derby winner at the age of 30, Genuine Risk is the main attraction at the 400-acre Newstead Farm as visitors journey to the farm each year during the Hunt Country Stable Benefit Tour.

Raise a Native's sire line has also had a great influence on the Quarter Horse, predominantly through his son Raise a Man who sired the brilliant Special Effort. Another signature chestnut with an elongated star and strip, Special Effort was produced in 1979 by the Double Devil mare Go Effortlessly, whose Thoroughbred dam Hijo Beauty was a daughter of the speedy Spotted Bull.

Special Effort's racing career will go down in the history books as one of the greatest of all time. He posted a 4 1/2-length win in the Kansas Futurity Trials, and continued the streak with victories in the Kansas Futurity and the Rainbow Futurity. Dominating the two-year-old Quarter Horse racing scene in 1981, Special Effort also won the coveted All American Futurity by 4 1/2 lengths over a muddy track. With that victory he became the first and only Quarter Horse to sweep the Triple Crown at Ruidoso Downs. He won divisional honors that year as the 1981 champion two-year-old stallion, champion two-year-old, and world champion.

Prior to retirement as a three-year-old, Special Effort won the Kansas Derby. He retired with 13 wins from 14 starts, earnings of $1,219,950 and a speed index of 104. Syndicated for a record $15 million, Special Effort etched a niche in history as the third leading active sire of all-time money earners, and has sired five American Quarter Horse Association racing champions.

Mr. Prospector, Raise a Native's most prolific son at stud, has earned the right to his own chapter. Arguably the most influential member of the Raise a Native clan to become a sire of sires into the 21st century, Mr. Prospector's legacy will be felt for generations through his sons Fappiano, Forty Niner, Crafty Prospector, Conquistador Cielo, Gone West, Miswaki, Fusaichi Pegasus, Seeking the Gold, Woodman, Gulch, Kingmambo, Machiavellian, and Carson City.

Soundness issues plagued Mr. Prospector throughout a relatively short racing career as a brilliantly fast sprinter. However he was bred to a wide array of mares with bloodlines containing a higher degree of stamina and soundness. As a result, his sire line has continued to branch out into classic performers throughout the world that are capable of a mile or better with that late closing kick of blinding Raise a Native speed.

The grand old man, his face peppered with gray hair handed down from his sire Native Dancer, was put down at Spendthrift Farm in July, 1988, due to spinal deterioration at the age of 27. Raise a Native's legacy will endure as long as there are racetracks to run on and records to break.

CHAPTER TEN

MAJESTIC PRINCE

When the copper-toned son of Raise a Native paraded into the Keeneland sales ring, all eyes were upon his glistening physique as the bidding escalated to a feverish pitch. Breeder Leslie Combs, glancing about the pavilion, was elated by the colt's popularity. There was no doubting near perfection. The colt was darn near flawless and the bidders knew it.

The hammer fell on a record-setting $250,000 for the stunning chestnut colt, purchased by Canadian industrialist Frank McMahon. Aptly named Majestic Prince, the colt's racing career was almost as peerless as his sales-topping conformation.

"He has looks, he has speed, he has courage," Combs recalled in an interview with *Time* magazine before the 1969 Kentucky Derby. "And most important, he has done everything right from the start."

Majestic Prince was out of stakes-placed Your Hostess, a full sister to the speedy but ill-fated Santa Anita Derby winner and sire Your Host, by Alibhai. His second dam was the prolific Boudoir II, a gray daughter of Mahmoud, acquired by Combs in 1948 from MGM mogul Louis B. Mayer.

From the onset there was no denying "the Prince."

McMahon sent Majestic Prince to Hall of Fame jockey and trainer Johnny Longden in California to begin his racing career. Longden, who retired as the world's winningest jockey in 1966, had ridden Count Fleet to victory in all three Triple Crown races. He also became the only trainer in history to ride and train a Kentucky Derby winner.

Majestic Prince streaks for home in the 1969 Kentucky Derby.

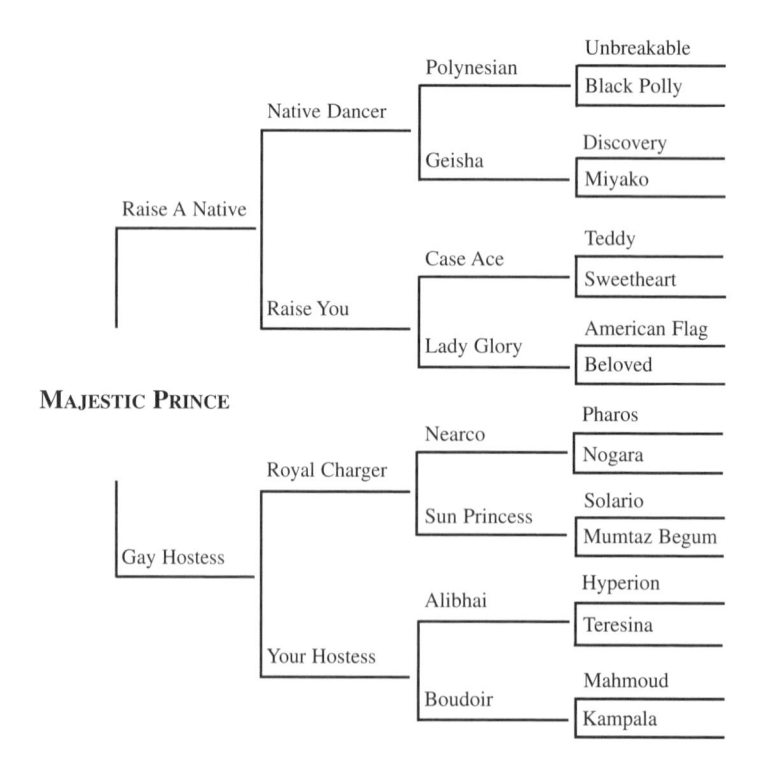

MAJESTIC PRINCE

- Raise A Native
  - Native Dancer
    - Polynesian
      - Unbreakable
      - Black Polly
    - Geisha
      - Discovery
      - Miyako
  - Raise You
    - Case Ace
      - Teddy
      - Sweetheart
    - Lady Glory
      - American Flag
      - Beloved
- Gay Hostess
  - Royal Charger
    - Nearco
      - Pharos
      - Nogara
    - Sun Princess
      - Solario
      - Mumtaz Begum
  - Your Hostess
    - Alibhai
      - Hyperion
      - Teresina
    - Boudoir
      - Mahmoud
      - Kampala

In his fall campaign as a two-year-old in 1968, the lightly raced Majestic Prince won his only two races that year. He returned to action as a three-year-old with a powerful and strapping physique, topping out at 1,120 pounds of sheer lightning speed.

With jockey Bill Hartack in the irons, Majestic Prince became the dominant factor on the West Coast with victories in the 1969 San Vincente, Los Feliz, and San Jacinto Stakes. His scintillating eight-length win in the 1969 Santa Anita Derby solidified McMahon's desire to send him to Louisville as an undefeated contender for the Kentucky Derby.

The field for the 95th running of the Kentucky Derby was the smallest in the history of the race with only eight horses parading to the starting gate. Majestic Prince was the betting favorite with seven straight victories, while champion two-year-old Top Knight was the second favorite. Claiborne Farm's highly touted Dike was the third choice, with Paul Mellon's classy chestnut colt Arts and Letters following as the fourth betting pick.

Longden, who had recommended the purchase of Majestic Prince as a yearling to McMahon, remarked on Hartack's belief in the colt in an interview with *Time* prior to the Derby.

"Hartack is so high on this colt he comes out to work him in the mornings, and you know how many name jocks do that," Longden said.

Breaking from the last post position on the far outside, Majestic Prince galloped along easily as Arts and Letters glided down the rail to snatch the lead at the mile marker. On the turn for home, Majestic Prince charged up alongside Arts and Letters from the outside and dug in for the drive. Battling gamely down the stretch, Mellon's game contender could not hold off Majestic Prince as he pulled away to win the Derby by a neck. A trio of personal milestones were achieved that day as the victory gave Combs, as breeder, his first and only Kentucky Derby winner, Longden became the first trainer to ride and train a Derby victor, and Majestic Prince became the first unbeaten Derby winner in 47 years.

The media conjured up a rivalry between "The Prince" and Arts and Letters following the Derby victory, which led to a second meeting in the Preakness Stakes at Pimlico Racecourse.

Majestic Prince, heavily favored in the Preakness, repeated the gutsy duel with Arts and Letters and won by a head. It appeared that "The Prince" was well on his way to becoming the first Triple Crown winner since Citation in 1948.

Leading up to the 1969 Belmont Stakes, Combs attributed a degree of Majestic Prince's success to a pellet ration developed by the Trappist Monks at Gesthemane in an article in the June 4, 1969 *Miami Herald*: "If Majestic Prince wins Saturday's Belmont Stakes for racing's Triple Crown, part of the credit can go to the Trappist monks in a monastery near Bardstown, Kentucky. Leslie Combs II, who bred the Prince and sold him to Frank McMahon as a yearling, explains he feeds his young horses special pellets containing a secret formula that is made up each season to match blood samples of the new foals on Combs' farm. He once had a commercial firm make them for him, Combs said, but learned the firm was also selling over the counter to other horsemen. So, he turned to the monastery to make them. 'If you can't trust the monks, who can you trust?' Combs asks."

Following the Preakness, Longden discovered that Majestic Prince had a developing problem in his right front tendon. After much debate with McMahon, Longden said that the horse would not be at his best for the Belmont Stakes and would be shipped back to California in order to lay up for a fall campaign. McMahon backed up Longden's philosophy when he told a reporter "We want a Triple Crown, not a Crippled Crown."

The media frenzy that followed bombarded Longden with a flurry of questions and aggravation. Longden, a consummate horseman, found it difficult to explain to a non-horse-oriented media as to why a "developing" tendon problem resulted in circumstances that would cause Majestic Prince to bypass a stab at racing immortality.

Obviously the pressure got to McMahon, who made the decision to enter Majestic Prince in the Belmont in spite of the tendon issue. Much speculation has surrounded this decision, without any obvious or documented conclusion. Longden, disgusted and disgruntled after being overruled by McMahon, reluctantly sent Majestic Prince to the post in the Belmont with the knowledge that he was teetering on the brink of injury.

The stage for the Belmont was set in the most unusual fashion. Heavily favored Majestic Prince, with the knowledge of pending injury, was entered to make a bid for the Triple Crown in spite of Longden's belief that it was not in the colt's best interest. Arts and Letters' trainer, Elliott Burch, confident in his colt's soundness and stamina, had entered him in the Metropolitan Handicap at Aqueduct only a week prior to the Belmont. Arts and Letters won "the Met" convincingly, and cast an even longer shadow of doubt over the Majestic Prince camp.

In an uneventful start to an even more uneventful race, Dike scrambled to a five-length lead in the Belmont through dreadfully slow fractions. Arts and Letters, loping along with ease, found an opening and shot to the lead under the guidance of jockey Braulio Baeza. Hartack, apparently unconcerned by the pedestrian pace, made a bid for the lead entering the stretch but to no avail. Arts and Letters cruised under the wire to win the Belmont by 5 1/2 lengths, with Majestic Prince in second. He never raced again, and retired with nine wins from 10 starts, and earnings of $414,200.

Hartack later told reporters, "The horse was hurting. We should have never run in the Belmont."

Longden stated that Majestic Prince had injured his check ligament in the right front leg, and that the injury probably occurred when he bore out in the Preakness. McMahon's comments, if any, are unknown.

Following Majestic Prince's bid for the Triple Crown, Combs sold his full brother for a new record price of $510,000 that same year. The colt, named Crowned Prince, went on to become a champion two-year-old in England.

Retired to Spendthrift Farm, Combs syndicated Majestic Prince for $1.8 million. The stunning chestnut stallion retained his sales-topping good looks throughout his breeding career. He died in 1981 from an apparent heart attack at the age of 15. Majestic Prince sired 33 stakes winners, including 1979 Belmont Stakes winner and sire Coastal. In 1988, Majestic Prince was inducted into the Racing Hall of Fame.

The Kentucky Derby trophy won by Majestic Prince was purchased for $60,000 at the Doyle Auction in New York on July 20, 2005.

The purchaser was Secretariat.com, a company operated in part by Penny Chenery, owner of 1973 Triple Crown winner Secretariat. The under bidder for the coveted trophy was the Kentucky Derby Museum at Churchill Downs, which has one of the largest collections of Derby trophies on display. The trophy was featured in a 1969 Derby exhibit at the museum in 2005, which also contained the silks worn by Bill Hartack.

Leslie Combs had commissioned a duplicate of the gold trophy that displayed his name as the breeder of Majestic Prince. The Kentucky Derby Museum has the coveted Combs trophy on display to memorialize the brilliance of Majestic Prince.

Chapter Eleven

MR. PROSPECTOR

A balanced, bright bay yearling bred by Leslie Combs sauntered into the sales pavilion at Keeneland, and there was a hush among bidders as the announcer read off his aristocratic connections.

"Now here we have a yearling bay colt sired by the popular Raise a Native, out of the stakes winning Gold Digger...second in the Kentucky Oaks, look-a-here at this nice colt..."

The bidding needed no prompting. When the hammer fell on $220,000, breeder A.I. "Butch" Savin became the owner of the exquisitely made sales topper who would be named Mr. Prospector.

Mr. Prospector, foaled in 1970, was the result of the second of seven matings between the tough, stakes-winning Gold Digger and fragile Raise a Native. The first mating resulted in a winner who broke down as a two-year-old, the third had a breathing problem although he was stakes-placed, and the last four were perpetually unsound. Gold Digger did go on to produce stakes winners Lillian Russell (by Prince John) and Gold Standard (by Sea-Bird). But the genetic gold mine revealed the highest assay in Mr. Prospector.

Raise a Native was a lightning fast son of Native Dancer, out of the Case Ace mare Raise You. However he was not a sound horse, and his racing career came to a close in mid-July of his two-year-old year.

Raise a Native won over three furlongs, twice over five, and once over 5 1/2 furlongs. It was left to history to figure out just how good he really was. At the close of his career, Raise a Native was sent to Spendthrift Farm to begin his breeding career. His first crop unleashed a group of precocious and speedy two-year-olds, many with soundness issues. Mr. Prospector was not the exception. Savin was a Connecticut businessman and the owner of a stud farm in Florida. He had tasted success as the breeder of 1970 champion two-year-old filly Forward Gal, and realized that in order to get a top notch sire prospect he would have to race it himself. The top-notch Thoroughbreds inevitably retired to Kentucky to breed, and Florida was in need of a popular young sire.

Mr. Prospector was sent to trainer Jimmy Croll for conditioning, and Savin eagerly awaited good news on his expensive four-legged investment. After what seemed like an eternity, Croll reported back to Savin that Mr. Prospector came back shin sore every time he worked. As a result, "Mr. P" never raced as a juvenile.

In February of 1973, Mr. Prospector made his debut at Hialeah in a six-furlong maiden race, and won by an astounding 12 lengths. Two weeks later Croll entered him in an allowance race over seven furlongs and he sailed to a near six-length score.

Mr. Prospector missed the Grade 3 Hutcheson Stakes due to a fever, but it turned out to be a blessing in disguise. He returned to win a six-furlong allowance race at Gulfstream Park in a new track record time of 1:07 4/5.

With these kind of results, Savin got Kentucky Derby fever and sent Mr. Prospector to Kentucky. The performance was less than what he had hoped for. Mr. Prospector finished second in the one-mile Grade 3 Derby Trial Stakes at Churchill Downs, and returned to the shedrow with a chip in his off-fore fetlock. The injury kept him out of contention until February 1974.

Under Croll's watchful eye, Mr. Prospector returned to action and won an allowance race at Gulfstream Park by five lengths in speedy fashion. Savin was itching for a stakes-winning stallion prospect, and Croll knew that he had to make it happen. Mr. Prospector traveled to New York, and finished third in the Paumonok Handicap at Aqueduct.

After making the trip back to Miami for a second-place finish in the Royal Poinciana Handicap at Hialeah, Croll sent the son of Raise a Native to Garden State for a shot at the Whirlaway Handicap. Highweighted in the company of top-notch sprinters, Mr. Prospector galloped away with the Whirlaway in a new track record time of 1:08 3/5 for six furlongs. Ability overcame ambition when Mr. Prospector met Horse of the Year Forego in the Grade 2 Carter Handicap, finishing a far-outclassed second in the seven-furlong test.

As a four-year-old, Mr. Prospector moved up in class with a victory over the nation's top sprinters in the six-furlong Gravesend Handicap at Belmont Park. It was obvious that Mr. Prospector, as a maturing horse, was definitely improving.

It is seldom that soundness and speed compliment one another, and Mr. Prospector was no exception. Plagued with injury throughout his career, the game runner suffered a career-ending injury when he fractured a sesamoid during a workout at Monmouth Park on July 26, 1974. In a strange twist of irony, only four days earlier his full brother Kentucky Gold was sold at Keeneland by Combs for a then-world-record price of $625,000. Mr. Prospector was retired with seven wins from 14 starts, and earnings of $112,171. Savin had his stakes-winning stallion prospect.

Mr. Prospector became the resident stallion at Aisco Farm in Ocala, Florida, standing for the modest fee of $7,500. As a mature horse he stood at approximately 16 hands, was balanced and powerful, with a plain head, and turned out in the off-fore. Although well bred and speedy, Savin wondered if the colt could impart class into the sub par broodmare population that resided in Florida at the time. Mr. Prospector did not disappoint.

The first crop of Mr. P's hit the ground running. There were a mere 28 foals in his first crop, but from that group emerged four stakes winners including It's In the Air, honored as the 1978 co-champion two-year-old filly. As a result of her exploits, Mr. Prospector became the leading first crop sire that year, and began to raise eyebrows in Kentucky. The Mr. P's were fast, precocious, and defined class.

The following year, Mr. Prospector sired 51 foals and produced 11 stakes winners from that crop which endowed him with the title of the nation's leading sire of two-year-olds. The name of the hot, young, and upcoming sire on Kentuckian's lips was Mr. Prospector. Now the key was to get him there.

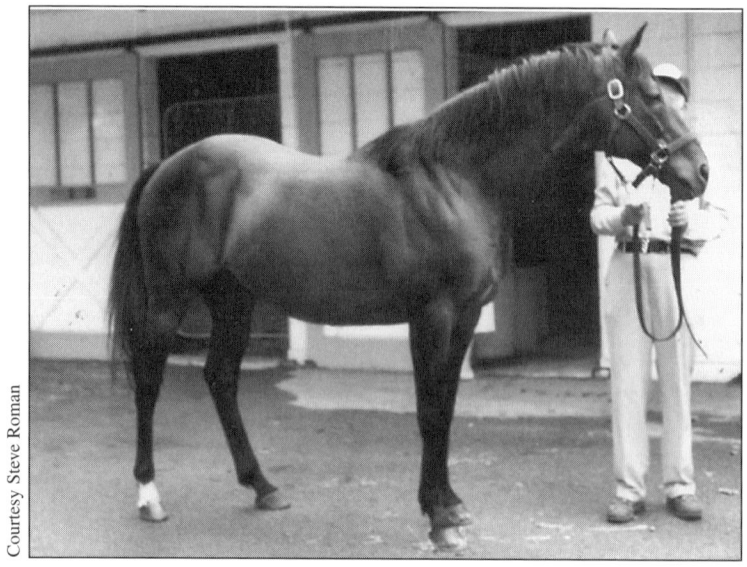

Mr. Prospector at Claiborne Farm.

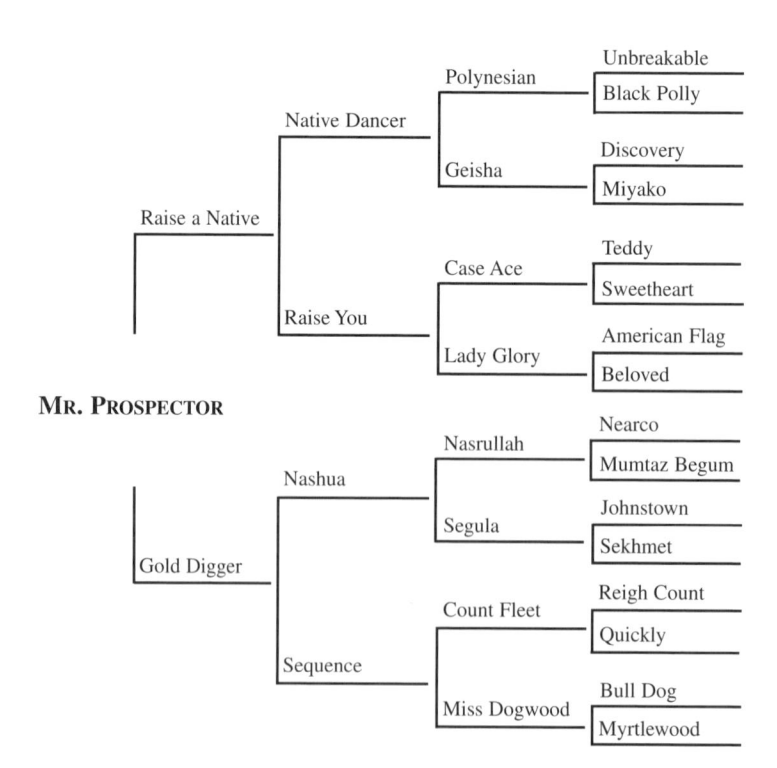

MR. PROSPECTOR

- Raise a Native
  - Native Dancer
    - Polynesian
      - Unbreakable
      - Black Polly
    - Geisha
      - Discovery
      - Miyako
  - Raise You
    - Case Ace
      - Teddy
      - Sweetheart
    - Lady Glory
      - American Flag
      - Beloved
- Gold Digger
  - Nashua
    - Nasrullah
      - Nearco
      - Mumtaz Begum
    - Segula
      - Johnstown
      - Sekhmet
  - Sequence
    - Count Fleet
      - Reigh Count
      - Quickly
    - Miss Dogwood
      - Bull Dog
      - Myrtlewood

Courtesy Steve Roman

Although it would have seemed a natural that Mr. Prospector would have returned to Spendthrift Farm to stand at stud it was Claiborne Farm that won big. When Mr. Prospector's third crop of foals hit the racetrack in 1980, his fee had escalated to $40,000. Mare owners in Florida found it difficult to dig that deep into their pockets. Savin asked Seth Hancock of Claiborne Farm if he would be interested in standing the popular young Raise a Native son at the Paris, Kentucky, farm. It did not take long to strike a deal, and at the closure of his sixth season at stud in Florida Mr. Prospector moved to Claiborne Farm for the remainder of his stud career. While standing in Florida, Mr. Prospector sired a total of 50 stakes winners, including classic winners and champions Hello Gorgeous, Conquistador Cielo, and Gold Beauty.

Mr. Prospector stood his first season at Claiborne for $100,000, and as his progeny came to dominate the turf on both sides of the Atlantic it continued to rise to $325,000 in 1986.

In 1987, Mr. Prospector led the North American sire's list with earnings of $5,877,385, and duplicated this feat in 1988 with $8,986,790 in progeny earnings. He also topped the leading sire of two-year-olds list three times, and became the leading sire of broodmares in 1997, 1998, and 1999. Mr. Prospector heads the all-time leading sire of stakes winners list with 172 and progeny earnings of $87 million from 903 starters and 692 winners (76.6 percent).

An interesting aspect regarding Mr. Prospector is that he has sired one winner of each Triple Crown race – 2000 Kentucky Derby winner and sire Fusaichi Pegasus, 1985 Preakness Stakes winner Tank's Prospect, and 1982 Belmont Stakes winner, sire, and Horse of the Year Conquistador Cielo. He has proven to be a multi-dimensional sire on both turf and dirt, imparting a rare blend of speed and stamina worldwide.

Mr. Prospector lived to the ripe old age of 29. He was euthanized due to complications following a bout of colic on June 1, 1999, at Claiborne Farm. He was still an active breeding stallion in his last days at Claiborne, and as of May 1, 1999, had 31 mares confirmed in foal from 45 booked to him in his 25th season at stud.

Mr. Prospector/principal stakes winners

Ravinella (dam by Northern Dancer), European 2yo champion, One Thousand Guineas (G1), Poule d'Essai des Pouliches (G1), Cheveley Park Stakes (G1).

Machiavellian (dam by Halo), European 2 yo champion; Prix de la Salamandre (G1).

Conquistador Cielo (dam by Bold Commander), Horse of the Year, Belmont Stakes (G1), Metropolitan Handicap (G1), etc.

Forty Niner (dam by Tom Rolfe), 2yo champion,Travers Stakes (G1), Champagne Stakes (G1), 2nd Kentucky Derby (G1), etc.

Gulch (dam by Rambunctious), champion sprinter, Breeders' Cup Sprint (G1).

Rhythm (dam by Northern Dancer), 2yo champion, Breeders' Cup Juvenile (G1).

Eillo (dam by Northern Dancer), champion sprinter, Breeders' Cup Sprint (G1).

Fusaichi Pegasus (dam by Danzig), Kentucky Derby (G1), Wood Memorial Stakes (G2), etc.

Golden Attraction (dam by Seattle Slew), 2yo filly champion, Frizette Stakes (G1), Matron Stakes (G1), Spinaway Stakes (G1), etc.

Queena (dam by Blushing Groom), champion older mare, Maskette Stakes (G1), Ruffian Handicap (G1),Ballerina Stakes (G1), etc.

It's In The Air (dam by Francis S.), 2yo filly champion, Vanity Handicap (G1) twice, Alabama Stakes (G1), etc.

Afleet (dam by Venetian Jester), Canadian Horse of the Year, Jerome Handicap (G1), Pennsylvania Derby (G2), etc.

Seeking the Gold (dam by Buckpasser), Super Derby (G1), Dwyer Stakes (G1), 2nd Breeders' Cup Classic (G1), etc.

Tanks Prospect (dam by Pretense), Preakness Stakes (G1), 2nd Breeders' Cup Juvenile (G1), etc.

Chester House (dam by El Gran Senor), Arlington Million (G1), Brigadier Gerard Stakes (G3), etc.

Additional Grade/Group winners:

Kingmambo	Lion Cavern
Coup De Genie	Carson City
Educated Risk	Damister
Gone West	Numerous
Carson City	Chequer
Mogambo	Faltaat
Fappiano	Crafty Prospector
Miswaki	Homebuilder
Lycius	Kayrawan
Scan	Souvenir Copy
Mining	Miesque's Son
Hello Gorgeous	Red Carnival
Smart Strike	Tersa
Ta Rib	Macoumba
Jade Hunter	Educated Risk
Miner's Mark	Cuddles
Distant View	Chic Chirine
Woodman	Classic Crown
Jade Robbery	Dance Sequence
Procida	Scoot
Smart Strike	Preach
Mogambo	Fantastic Find
Bellotto	

Major sons at stud:

Fappiano
Gone West
Seeking the Gold
Fusaichi Pegasus
Forty Niner
Gulch
Crafty Prospector
Carson City
Woodman
Kingmambo
Machiavellian

Bellotto
Secret Prospector
Conquistador Cielo
Afleet
Proclaim
Straight
Strike
Silver Ghost
Miswaki
Tale of the Cat

Broodmare sire of 179 stakes winners and counting

Hollywood Wildcat (Breeders' Cup Distaff [G1])
Dayjur (English Horse of the Year)
Dancehall (Grand Prix de Paris [G1])
Dowsing (Vernon Sprint Cup [G1])
Green Tune (French Two Thousand Guineas [G1])
Lahan (English One Thousand Guineas [G1])
Fasiliyev (Prix Morny [G1])
Event of the Year (Jim Beam Stakes [G2])
Fire the Groom (Beverly D Stakes [G1])
Finder's Fee (Matron Stakes [G1])
Pas De Response (champion two-year-old)
Geri (Oaklawn Handicap [G1])
Bint Allayl (Lowther Stakes [G2])
Tomisue's Delight (Personal Ensign Handicap [G1])
Maplejinsky (Alabama Stakes [G1])
Pulpit (Bluegrass Stakes [G2])
Accelerator (Pilgrim Stakes [G3])
Tale of the Cat (King's Bishop Stakes [G2])
Golden Opinion (Coronation Stakes [G1])
Sea of Secrets (San Vincente Stakes [G2])
Latin American (Californian Stakes [G1])

CHAPTER TWELVE

LANDALUCE

Turf writers and racing historians will continue to speculate on just how good Landaluce could have been. The undefeated champion daughter of Seattle Slew has been compared to the likes of Ruffian, and other outstanding distaff performers whose careers were tragically cut short. Her undaunted spirit and effortless power have remained etched in the memory of all who were lucky enough to watch her breathtaking stretch run.

Landaluce was a member of 1977 Triple Crown winner Seattle Slew's highly anticipated first crop of 1980. The striking dark bay or brown filly, bred by Leslie Combs in partnership with Francis Kernan, was foaled on April 11, 1980 to the 13-year-old Bold Bidder mare Strip Poker.

Following Seattle Slew's defeat to J.O. Tobin in the 1977 Swaps Stakes at Hollywood Park, the partnership of Brownell Combs, Washington lumberman Joe Layman, and Franklin Groves purchased a 50 percent interest in Seattle Slew from the Hills and Taylors for $3.5 million. Layman owned 50 percent of the partnership, while Brownell and Groves each retained 25 percent. The intent was to campaign Seattle Slew during his four-year-old year, and eventually retire the Triple Crown winner to stand at Spendthrift Farm.

"Seattle Slew was the most complete racehorse I've ever known," recalled Brownell. "He had it all – brains, courage, and raw racing talent. That horse could have trained himself."

After a 3 1/4-length win in the 1978 Stuyvesant Stakes, Seattle Slew was retired to Spendthrift and syndicated by Brownell for $12 million.

"Seattle Slew sold himself as a racehorse," Brownell said. "But his conformation did raise a few eyebrows regarding his potential as a stallion. He turned out so badly in the right fore that it looked like his leg was put on backwards. As it turned out, it didn't matter, and his two-year-olds ran like hell."

Breeders speculated on just how good the Slew babies could be as they watched the yearlings grow into reproductions of their hickory sire, whose coarseness had been handed down from his great grandsires Round Table and Hail to Reason. Some breeders were not game to take a chance on the conformational deviations of Seattle Slew, and gravitated toward another Spendthrift stallion whose arresting good looks could not be disputed.

J.O. Tobin, who defeated Seattle Slew in the 1978 Swaps Stakes, was a stunningly handsome and correct dark bay son of Never Bend purchased by Brownell and Nelson Bunker Hunt while still in training. Named the co-champion sprinter of 1978, J.O. Tobin sired elegant and aesthetically pleasing youngsters that emulated their handsome sire. When the first J.O. Tobin's hit the racetrack as two-year-olds in the same year as the Seattle Slew juveniles, there was no dispute. Hickory won hands down over handsome.

"The best Seattle Slew babies were put together just like him," recalled Brownell. "Most breeders were game to take a chance on a Triple Crown winner like Slew, but some were skeptical at first. The Slew babies were runners, and J.O. Tobin was a disappointment in the breeding shed. The rest is history."

Seattle Slew's first crop was nothing short of phenomenal. From that first batch emerged champions Landaluce and Slew o' Gold, and Grade 1 winners Adored and Slewpy. In his second crop came ill-fated Kentucky Derby winner Swale, and Grade 1 winners Seattle Song and Tsunami Slew.

The brilliance and tenacity of Seattle Slew happened to be the perfect match for the Bold Bidder mare Strip Poker.

Strip Poker was retired to the broodmare band after a lackluster second-place finish in one of two starts as a two-year-old. Prior to Landaluce, Strip Poker produced seven foals including the Grade 3 winner Clout, by *Indian Chief, and French Group 3-placed In Tissar, by Roberto. Her pedigree carried a high degree of stamina, with inbreeding to Blenheim II's dam Malva in the fourth and fifth generations. Landaluce is also inbred in the third and fourth generations to Bold Ruler through Seattle Slew's sire Bold Reasoning, and her damsire Bold Bidder.

Several branches of Landaluce's female family have continued with success. Strip Poker's daughter Our Bidder became the great-grandam of the speedy stakes winner and Grade 3-placed Baldomera, by Doneraile Court. Royal Strait Flush, a full sister to Landaluce, produced Grade 2 winner Jade Flush, and is the grandam of Grade 1 winner Startac. Farther removed members of the immediate female family include champion grass horse, Breeders' Cup Turf winner, and sire Theatrical, champion grass horse Paradise Creek, and Grade 1 winners Wild Event and Forbidden Apple.

Landaluce, like all the other Spendthrift yearlings in 1981, was prepped for the Keeneland September yearling sales. The filly's athleticism, deep heartgirth, and presence caught the eye of trainer D. Wayne Lukas, who purchased her for $650,000 as agent for Larry French and Barry Beall.

Lukas was a leading Quarter Horse trainer who had made the switch to Thoroughbreds with a high degree of success right from the start. In 1977, Lukas took owners French, Beall, and Mel Hatley with him into Thoroughbred ownership, and purchased eventual champion Terlingua for $275,000 at Keeneland. He won the 1980 Preakness Stakes with Codex, and trained his first Derby starter in 1980 with Partez. Lukas was emerging as an astute trainer of Thoroughbreds, a razor-sharp businessman, and a gifted horseman with a sixth sense. He proved a perfect choice to condition Landaluce.

The special connection between Lukas and Landaluce was apparent right from the start. She trained like a giant, and he knew she was something special. There was no disputing the fact that the two-year-old filly was talented. Perhaps only Lukas really knew how expansive her brilliance truly was.

Fireworks followed Landaluce in her maiden bow on July 3, 1982, at Hollywood Park. Hustling to the lead through opening quarters

Courtesy Shigeki Kikkawa

Landaluce at Santa Anita

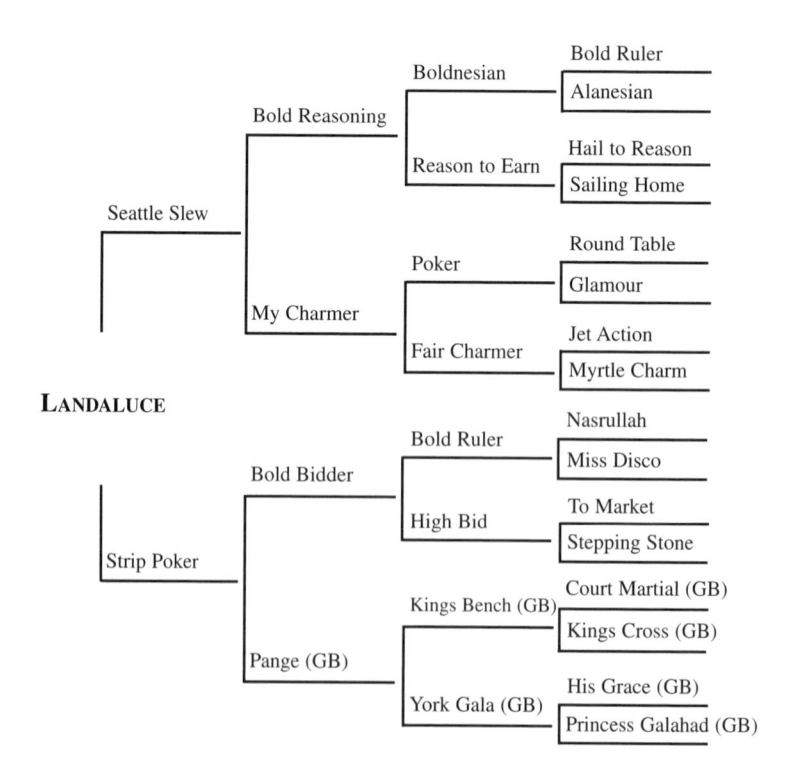

LANDALUCE
- Seattle Slew
  - Bold Reasoning
    - Boldnesian
      - Bold Ruler
      - Alanesian
    - Reason to Earn
      - Hail to Reason
      - Sailing Home
  - My Charmer
    - Poker
      - Round Table
      - Glamour
    - Fair Charmer
      - Jet Action
      - Myrtle Charm
- Strip Poker
  - Bold Bidder
    - Bold Ruler
      - Nasrullah
      - Miss Disco
    - High Bid
      - To Market
      - Stepping Stone
  - Pange (GB)
    - Kings Bench (GB)
      - Court Martial (GB)
      - Kings Cross (GB)
    - York Gala (GB)
      - His Grace (GB)
      - Princess Galahad (GB)

116

of :22 and :44 3/5, under the guidance of Laffit Pincay, Jr., Landaluce remained unchallenged throughout as she stretched her margin to an easy seven-length win in a sharp 1:08 1/5 for six furlongs over a fast track.

"This is a fast filly, and we have nothing but the highest regard for her," Lukas told a reporter prior to the 1982 Hollywood Lassie on July 10. "There is no guessing on how good she could really be...sky's the limit."

Zipping through early fractions of :21 3/5 and :43 4/5, Landaluce shot to the lead with precision and unleashed her powerful acceleration with flawless execution. Leading by nine lengths entering the stretch, Landaluce destroyed the field with an effortless 21-length romp in a swift 1:08 for the six-furlong distance, with Bold Out Line trailing in second, and Barzell in third. It was the longest margin of victory ever recorded for a stakes win at Hollywood Park. Truly, the sky was the limit.

Landaluce returned from a seven-week freshening to make her third start in the Del Mar Debutante at Del Mar on September 5. It was the Seattle Slew filly's first start over the mile distance, but Lukas and her connections were more than confident. In her signature style, Landaluce gained command, and kicked clear to score by 6 1/2 lengths in 1:35 3/5, just three-fifths of a second off the stakes record set by Table Hands.

On October 11, Landaluce made her fourth start in the seven-furlong Anoakia Stakes at Santa Anita Park. Slicing through rivals to nab the lead, Landaluce powered to a 10-length win in 1:21 4/5. The undefeated Seattle Slew filly needed a Grade 1 win to add to her blossoming resume, and the Oak Leaf Stakes on October 23 at the Arcadia oval was the perfect test.

Making her first start over 1 1/16 miles, Landaluce scampered to the lead through quick quarters of :22 3/5 and :44 4/5. Sophisticated Girl attempted to throw down a challenge, but Landaluce rebuffed that rival to win by two lengths in 1:41 4/5.

Landaluce was scheduled to make her sixth start in the Hollywood Starlet on November 22. However, fate delivered a heart-wrenching blow that stunned the racing world with its untimely outcome.

On the day of what might have been her sixth straight victory, Landaluce became ill with the life-threatening bacterial infection colitis.

Lukas, ever present, remained by her side throughout the week as veterinarians desperately tried to save her life. Her condition steadily declined in spite of the valiant efforts to save the courageous filly. Landaluce died on November 28 with her head cradled in Lukas' lap. She was buried on December 12, 1982, in the infield of Hollywood Park, the site of her most illustrious 21-length victory.

"I wouldn't feel this badly if my own son died," said a grieving Lukas in an interview shortly after the death of Landaluce.

Landaluce was named the first California-based Eclipse award-winning two-year-old filly in 1982, and Seattle Slew went on to lead the American sire list in 1984. Landaluce became the first in a long string of champions for Lukas, who conditioned such greats as Thunder Gulch, Winning Colors, Lady's Secret, Flanders, Azeri, and Serena's Song among many.

Chapter Thirteen

BREEDING A GOOD HORSE

The Combs philosophy on breeding a good horse was as much a part of his award-winning recipe for success as the "Spendthrift spring water" that bubbled up from the black Kentucky soil. It was based on old fashioned horsemanship, razor-sharp business acumen, and an ability to speculate on current and future trends in racing and pedigree. Combs did not implement the aid of a computer, measuring devices, mathematical equations, speed figures, astrological charts, or graphs to measure the intangible – he gambled on it and won.

In 1969 the Jockey Club began researching the use of computer technology to aid breeders in choosing appropriate matings for Thoroughbreds. Combs, a member of the elite organization, was not convinced that computers could predict the potential outcome of a specific mating between sire and dam. The Jockey Club's research, which eventually evolved into their computerized pedigree and racing database, has since become an indispensable tool for horsemen worldwide.

When asked by a newspaper whether computerized mating would have been any help in arranging the mating between Raise A Native and Gay Hostess that produced Kentucky Derby winner Majestic Prince, Combs was logical in his assessment.

"The sire only raced four times, and the mare never started, so I don't know anything the computer could have told us," he asserted. "Five of the most important things about a champion racehorse you can't feed into a computer. That's class, intelligence, conformation, courage, and soundness. Conformation and soundness are evident to the eye, but the other three factors are completely intangible. When it comes to breeding horses, a computer takes the romance out of it."

Each individual was judged on its own merit based on race record, pedigree, conformation, and assessed potential – as a sire, dam, racehorse, or sales investment. Combs didn't dismiss the horse with a deviation in conformation or denote a specific physical type as the prototype of perfection. He left room for possibility with an open-minded approach to each individual's pre-ordained form to function. Many of the youngsters with less than perfect conformation were retained by Combs for the racing stable, and went on to become successful stakes winners in spite of their physical shortcomings.

"Many of the fillies that we race are less than perfect physically," Combs said in a 1967 interview. "However their bloodlines are superior, many of them tracing back to Myrtlewood, La Troienne, and other taproot mares. Racing ability is an intangible. Just because a horse isn't a perfect physical specimen doesn't mean it can't run. If you have the blood and the ability the rest will follow. We try to enhance that at Spendthrift."

Combs' speculation on the quality of a foal began at the moment of its birth. He would often stand and watch a foal for an hour or more after foaling, which allowed him to determine a great deal about the youngster's personality.

"You simply don't know where a good horse will come from," Combs said in an interview with the *Morning Telegraph* in 1971. "They come in all shapes and sizes. One of my pet theories in choosing a likely good horse begins at the beginning, or when he is foaled. The youngsters who survive the birth most quickly, and are up and around looking for worlds to conquer, they're my type of colt. Majestic Prince was that type of colt. He was up and around in 20 minutes, while others sometimes require twice or three times that amount of time. The same was true of Crowned Prince and some of the other good ones. It seems that they begin to show intelligence and determination from the minute they see the light of day.

"Many try to determine the top ones from the ordinary by the manner in which they play in the fields and how they engage in races against each other," Combs continued. "I don't subscribe to this, even though I can't help but marvel at the superiority of one over the others. You see there are periods of great transition in a young horse. That's why

I prefer to form opinions during the first few hours of their existence, it is then they show class. Later, like humans, they begin to grow and sometimes get all out of sorts. They're either too fat or too thin, and they develop all sorts of things, even ugly pimples. But later they return to the general appearance of their days as a suckling."

Nashua became the object of near physical perfection for Combs when choosing a stallion. Not only was the bay son of Nasrullah sound and his conformation predominantly correct, but his racing ability was superior along with his pedigree.

"You take Nashua," Combs told the *Saturday Evening Post*. "So many horses are spindly and not good in the girth. Nashua, he's a big stout horse, powerful everywhere, good head, good neck and shoulders and powerful hindquarters. He's got that look of eagles. Then you look to see if he's sound, if his legs are straight, and his ankles are set at a normal degree and if he moves easy – like a country boy on his way home from school."

Combs was an innovator who promoted the evolution of commercialism in the Thoroughbred business. He recognized that the yearling market was whimsical and trendy, and followed the necessary marketing strategies in order to deliver the latest fashion on four legs. The mares that he chose possessed a marketable pedigree which enhanced the probable sales success of their offspring. Stakes winners or mares with classic stakes-producing pedigrees and excellent conformation populated the paddocks at Spendthrift.

"We have several considerations to take into account," Combs recalled in a 1966 interview with the *Thoroughbred Record*. "First of all we try to follow the pattern of successful matings of the past. Some blood nicks very well with another cross, and once this has been proven on the racetrack, it is a good idea to follow along.

"Then we take conformation into account. You want to have a certain compatibility in conformation between sire and dam or you produce a freak. We also try to breed out faults at Spendthrift. We try to get favorable characteristics of the parents reproduced in the offspring. Speed and stamina are important in the pedigree to replicate a horse capable of navigating a classic distance with a late closing burst of speed.

"Quality mares are the foundation of a great stud farm. Look at the money Warren Wright spent when he was building up the Calumet Farm broodmare empire. That's why I've paid top prices for mares. It doesn't make sense to me to spend $10,000 for a stud fee, and then send a $5,000 mare to that stallion hoping for the best."

The Combs philosophy was evident in the quality of broodmares that resided in the pastures at Spendthrift beginning with the blue hen Myrtlewood and her descendants. He believed in mingling the best bloodlines from throughout the world, and would often purchase stakes-winning mares from Europe, Australia, and South America in order to introduce less utilized bloodlines into American stock. Combs employed genetic diversity by blending the best speed and stamina from top-class mares and stallions from a variety of countries.

"It doesn't matter where she's from, Timbuctoo, Taiwan, or Texas," Combs told *Turf and Sport Digest* in 1962. "But a good mare needs to have won stakes or come from a stakes-producing family. If the dam won stakes, the grandam, and great grandam, (won stakes) all the better. I also look for mares sired by proven stallions or stallions that were champions at the track. If you have a well-bred filly, she doesn't have to be a good racehorse. The mare who has never raced might still be the mother of a champion."

Combs usually kept and raced only fillies, including those that were not accepted to the Keeneland Select Sales. Alert Princess, Lady Tramp, and Gold Digger were several that were descended from Myrtlewood, but were also considered sale rejects.

"Gold Digger, that is one we're glad we kept," Combs said. "There's not much you could do wrong there. Raise a Native showed us that."

Notable Spendthrift Mares

*Source Sucree, 1940, by *Admiral Drake
out of Lavendula, by Pharos

Lavendula, the dam of Source Sucree, was culled from Lord Derby's prestigious herd of broodmares, and purchased for 750 guineas by Mr. Benjamin Guinness in 1933. Lavendula was a winner in three races in France, and raced without success in two English Handicaps. However, her offspring would cross the ocean on more than one occasion, and leave a lasting influence on pedigrees worldwide – predominantly through her son Ambiorix (who led the American sire list in 1961) and daughters Source Sucree and Perfume II (the dam of My Babu).

As a racehorse, Source Sucree won only one race from two starts in France. For what she lacked on the racecourse, she more than made up for as a broodmare.

Source Sucree was bred to Royal Charger prior to his importation from Ireland, and produced her sixth foal, a strapping bay colt, in 1951. The youngster, eventually named Turn-To, was imported to the United States by Claude Tanner and purchased by A.B. Hancock for $20,000 following Tanner's untimely death.

As a two-year-old, Turn-To showed a high degree of brilliance by winning the Saratoga Special and the Garden State Stakes, which was the richest race in America at the time. He notched three straight victories as a three-year-old, including the Flamingo Stakes, and became highly touted as the early favorite for the 1954 Kentucky Derby. Fate would not deliver, and Turn-To bowed a tendon leading up to the Derby and was retired.

Turn-To with George Darrer up, at Keeneland, with Ed Hayward, trainer.

Courtesy Keeneland Association, Meadors Collection

As a sire, Turn-to was first rate. In his first crop he produced First Landing, a crack juvenile performer, who won divisional honors as the 1958 champion two-year-old with victories in the 1958 Saratoga Special, Hopeful, and Garden State Stakes. A durable and consistent racehorse throughout his career, First Landing won 19 of 37 starts with earnings of $779,577. He also went on to sire 1974 Kentucky Derby and Preakness winner Riva Ridge.

Turn-to was also the sire of the 1960 champion two-year-old and successful sire Hail to Reason, winner of the Hopeful Stakes. He died in 1973.

Cagire II was the third foal produced by Source Sucree, and her second most noteworthy offspring. The bay colt by Tourbillon was foaled in 1947. Cagire II showed top form as a two-year-old when he finished second in the 1949 Duke of Edinburgh Stakes in his second start. As a three and four-year-old, he won the King George VI, Warren and Ormonde Stakes, and also finished third in the Princess of Wales's Stakes.

Moderately successful as a sire, Cagire II was exported to America in 1953, the same year as Source Sucree.

Source Sucree produced 13 foals, 10 starters, and nine winners including the Black Devil filly Black Brook, the brown colt Sourcillon by Pou du Ciel, and the colt Up All Hands, by All Hands.

Busher, 1942, by War Admiral, out of Baby League, by Bubbling Over

Busher's dam was the winning Bubbling Over daughter Baby League, whose dam was the great foundation mare La Troienne. She was bred in the purple from the very start, being a half sister to two-time American champion Bimelech and his full sister champion Black Helen (by Black Toney) and a full sister to stakes winner Biologist.

The daughters of Baby League were grand producers, namely Striking (a full sister to Busher), Glamour (the dam of multiple stakes winner Poker, and the grandam of champion Numbered Account), Sparkling (the dam of Grade 1 winner and sire Effervescing), La Dauphine (the grandam of Grade 1 winner and sire Obraztsovy) and Bases

Full (the grandam of Grade 1 winner Basie and stakes-winning sire Irish Open).

Busher, with Eddie Arcaro up. Blazingly fast, Busher was named champion two-year-old of 1944.

Owned and bred by Colonel Edward R. Bradley's Idle Hour Stock Farm near Lexington, Busher received the standard moniker beginning with a "B" given to all the Bradley horses. Bradley wasn't too keen on breeding Baby League to 1937 Triple Crown winner War Admiral due to the "hot blood" of the Fair Play sire line. He finally gave in to the idea when reminded how much War Admiral resembled the great racehorse and sire Sweep.

Busher, precocious and blazingly fast, was named the champion two-year-old of 1944.

Under the conditioning of former jockey Jimmy Smith, she racked up victories in the Selima and Matron Stakes, and the Adirondack Handicap.

The racing bans that followed the close of World War II did not halt Busher's brilliance, but may have only redirected its course during an abbreviated season.

James F. Byrnes, the director of War Mobilization and Reconversion, issued a statement on December 22, 1944, that requested the suspension of horse racing throughout the United States.

The statement read: "The operation of racetracks not only requires the employment of manpower needed for more essential operations, but also manpower, railroad transportation, as well as tires and gasoline in the movement of patrons to and from the track, and in the movement of horses...the existing war situation demands the utmost effort that the people of the United States can give...the operation of racetracks is not conducive to this all-out effort. Therefore, with the approval of the President, I urge that the management of these tracks take immediate measures to bring the present race meetings to a close by January 3, 1945...I am confident that the management...can be depended upon to take action without the necessity of recourse to other measures."

The announcement just happened to follow the surprise offensive attack by the Germans in the Ardennes Forest, and the counterattack by the Americans at the Battle of the Bulge. During the winter of 1944, the only racetracks that were open and operating included Tropical Park, Fair Grounds, and Sportsman's Park. On January 2, 1945, racing came to an absolute standstill in the United States.

Germany surrendered to the allies on May 7, and the documents were signed on May 8. The following day, Thoroughbred racing resumed in the United States, in spite of a ban on the transport of racehorses that remained in place until the Japanese surrender in August.

Bradley, who was in his eighties, realized that it was time to sell some horses, and sold Busher to movie mogul Louis B. Mayer for a reported $50,000 in March of her three-year-old year. In spite of the limitations in travel, Busher campaigned in Mayer's French blue and pink silks with eventual Hall of Fame jockey Johnny Longden in the irons and under the watchful eye of trainer George Odom.

The game filly won an allowance race at Santa Anita on May 26 by five lengths, and returned with a sharp seven-length score in the Santa Susana Stakes. In her first start against colts, Busher nabbed the San Vincente Stakes by 1 1/4 lengths in spite of being hampered by Quick Reward, who lost his rider and bounced around all over the racetrack.

In the Santa Margarita Handicap on July 4, Busher was co-highweight at 126 and easily defeated her stablemate Whirlabout. Three weeks later in Chicago, she won the female division of the Cleopatra Handicap, and returned on August 4 to nab the Arlington Handicap over older males.

Busher had finished third to the talented filly Durazna in the Beverly Handicap carrying 128 pounds. The plucky War Admiral filly was not about to be outdone. On August 29, Busher and Durazna met again in a match race carrying equal weights. Storming down the stretch, the two fillies battled for the lead in a game display. Digging in with tenacity, Busher would not be refuted, and charged past Durazna to win by three-quarters of a length.

Where gameness and courage were required, Busher could not be denied. On September 3, Calumet Farm's mighty track-record-setting gelding Armed met Busher in the Washington Park Handicap. Carrying 115 pounds to Armed's 120, Busher galloped away to a 1 1/2-length victory, and set a track record time of 2:01 4/5 for the 1 1/4-mile distance.

Busher added wins in the Hollywood Derby and Vanity Handicap prior to taking a year off due to a filling in her leg. She was the unanimous choice as the 1945 champion three-year-old filly, champion handicap mare, and Horse of the Year. She attempted to return to racing as a five-year-old, but without success. Busher retired with 15 wins, three seconds, one third in 21 starts, and earnings of $334,035.

At the culmination of her racing career, Busher was purchased by Neil McCarthy for $150,000 in Mayer's well-staged 1947 auction of 60 racehorses that realized the substantial sum of $1,553,500. Busher was again sold privately in 1948 to cosmetics entrepreneur Elizabeth Arden, and came to reside at Spendthrift and Maine Chance Farms for the duration of her short career as a broodmare.

Jet Action, by Jet Pilot, was the only stakes winner produced by Busher. A foal of 1951, Jet Action duplicated his mother's racing prowess by winning the Washington Park and Roamer Handicaps, and the Withers Stakes among 11 victories.

Busher's first foal was the 1949 Alibhai filly Miss Busher. Although not a stakes producer, she became the grandam of Alberta Derby winner Pilot Bird, and stakes winners Gemini Six and Agogo II. Popularity, a full sister to Miss Busher, produced the stakes winners Top Charger, Bevy of Roses, and Red Tulip, the great grandam of Italian Group 2 winner Come On Sassa. Bush Pilot, a full sister to Jet Action foaled in 1952, produced stakes winner Needle and Ball, and stakes-placed Level Flight. She became the grandam of stakes winner Five Star General, and Super Pleasure.

Sadly, Busher died shortly after the birth of her fifth foal, an unraced filly by Jet Pilot named Golden Heart.

Miss Request, 1945, by Requested, out of Throttle Wide, by Flying Heels

As a two-year-old in 1947, Miss Request scored only one win from 11 starts. She returned mature and fresh at the start of her three-year-old year, and won or placed in 13 of 20 starts. Her scintillating victories in the Ladies and Busher Handicaps and the Delaware Oaks garnered the champion three-year-old filly honors for 1948.

As a four-year-old, Miss Request won three of 20 starts, including the 1949 Beldame Handicap. She returned to the racetrack as a five-year-old, and lost three starts prior to retirement. Overall, she won 12 career starts with six second and five thirds over four seasons for earnings of $202,730.

As a broodmare, Miss Request produced a bevy of youngsters without much talent or durability. From eight foals, she produced all fillies, and had seven starters and four winners. Early in her life as a broodmare she was bred to some of the best stallions of the time, producing Laquesta, by War Admiral and the winning Jet Pilot daughter Shelly Jo.

Siama, 1947, by Tiger (by Bull Dog), out of China Face, by Display

Siama was a member of Harry Guggenheim's powerful Cain Hoy Stable and accumulated an impressive string of victories that only enhanced her potential as a broodmare. Over three seasons, Siama scored nine wins, including the Acorn and Jasmine Stakes, Comely Handicap, Monmouth Oaks, and Princess Doreen Stakes.

Honored as the 1960 Broodmare of the Year, Siama produced three stakes-winning sons and one champion from the full brothers One-Eyed King and Bald Eagle, by Nasrullah, and Dead Ahead, by Turn-To.

One-Eyed King, foaled in 1954, was Siama's second foal. From age two to six, the plucky colt blazed new track records and equaled old ones. He won the Donn Handicap twice, and scored in the Arlington, Long Island, and Magic City Handicaps among his 15 victories.

Siama's second mating to Nasrullah produced Bald Eagle. A tough and versatile racehorse in England and the United States, Bald Eagle was named the 1960 champion handicap horse after a dramatic campaign that included victories in the Washington D.C. International and Widener and Metropolitan Handicaps. He set a new track record of 1 1/4 miles in 1:59.60 in the Widener and returned to set a new track record for a mile in 1:33.60 in the Met. Bald Eagle also displayed his versatility on two continents with victories in the Craven, Duke of Edinburgh, and Dante Stakes in England.

Bald Eagle retired with 12 wins from two to five, and earnings of $692,946. As a stallion, he was syndicated for $1.4 million, and became a successful sire and broodmare sire. He was sent to France after standing in America for 11 years. The filly Too Bald became Bald Eagle's most notable offspring as the dam of Grand Prix de Paris and French St. Leger winner and sire Exceller.

Siama's sixth foal was the unraced Double Jay mare Whistle a Tune who was the dam of multiple Mexican champion Batucada, in turn the dam of multiple Irish group winner and sire Damister and Grade 1 winner and sire Selous Scout.

In 1959, Siama foaled a Turn-to colt that became her third and final stakes winner. Dead Ahead won the Roamer Handicap and set a new track record at Belmont Park for seven furlongs in 1:21.60.

Siama produced nine foals, three stakes winners, and five winners during her career as a broodmare. She died in 1965.

Straight Deal, 1962,
by Hail to Reason, out of No Fiddling, by King Cole

Straight Deal's talented and lengthy racing career emerged out of a decade filled with a myriad of racing's greatest stars. The popularity of Thoroughbred racing bloomed in the 1960's, and the enthusiastic crowds flocked to racetracks to cheer on the likes of Kelso, Dr. Fager, Northern Dancer, Buckpasser, and Damascus.

Hirsch Jacobs, seeking broodmare prospects tracing to La Troienne, claimed No Fiddling for $7,500 at Saratoga. The daughter of King Cole was unable to win a race, so Bieber retired her to the broodmare band. Straight Deal was the eighth foal produced by No Fiddling. Raced by the Bieber (Isidor)-Jacobs Stable, Straight Deal won two of eight starts as a juvenile. As a three-year-old in 1965, she notched her first two stakes victories in the Ladies Handicap at Aqueduct and the Hollywood Oaks at Hollywood Park out of 24 starts that year. From 20 starts at four, the tough little bay mare snatched four stakes wins in the Santa Margarita, Sheepshead Bay, Firenze, and Santa Barbara Handicaps.

Although not the epitome of consistency, Straight Deal was the model of durability. She clinched honors as the 1967 champion older mare at five with victories in the Delaware and Santa Margarita Handicaps, and the Spinster Stakes. From 22 starts that year, she won eight, finished second in five, and third in three. She also won back to back editions of the Bed O' Roses Handicap in 1966-67.

Straight Deal raced as a six- and seven-year-old, but with limited success. She finished second in the 1968 Barbara Fritchie and Gallorette Handicaps, but never won a stakes race again.

She retired with 21 wins (13 stakes), 21 seconds, and nine third place finishes out of 99 starts over six seasons. Twenty three of her placings were in stakes company. She retired in 1969 after remaining winless in three starts. Her career earnings of $733,020 were the second-highest earnings by a member of her gender at that time.

The great taproot mare La Troienne was Straight Deal's third dam, so it is no wonder that she was as prolific in the breeding shed as she was on the turf. The matings between Raise a Native or Raise a Native-line sons proved consistently magical when Straight Deal and her daughters were bred to them, and consistently produced talented racehorses, broodmares, and sires.

Desiree, Straight Deal's second foal, proved her merit on the racetrack by winning the Santa Barbara Handicap (G1). As a broodmare, the daughter of Raise a Native produced two-time Grade 1 winner Adored, by Seattle Slew, and Grade 3 winner Compassionate, by Housebuster.

Reminiscing was the third foal out of Straight Deal. Although she never won a graded stakes race, the daughter of Never Bend added three stakes victories to her resume by winning the Sequoia Handicap and La Potranca and La Habra Stakes. Her produce included three sons and one grandson of Exclusive Native that were all stakes winners or stakes-placed – Grade 2 winner Persevered (by Exclusive Native); stakes winner Premiership (by Exclusive Native); Commemorate, second in the Breeders' Cup Sprint (G1) (by Exclusive Native); and stakes-placed Sovereignty (by Affirmed).

Straight Deal's foal of 1978, So Endearing, by Raise a Native, produced Grade 1 winner Qualify. She is also the grandam of Grade 3 winner Notoriety, by Affirmed.

Belonging, by Exclusive Native, was foaled by Straight Deal in 1979. Although she won the Typecast Stakes and placed in two others, her legacy will endure as the dam of the speedy Grade 3 stakes winner and sire Belong To Me, by Danzig. She is also the grandam of Grade 3 winners Skipaslew and Away.

The winning Straight Deal daughter Affirmatively, by Affirmed, produced four influential daughters. Mais Oui, by Lyphard, won the Group 3 Prix de Sandringham, and produced Grade 2 winner Imperfect World, Grade 2-placed stakes winner and sire Monsieur Cat, and stakes-winning sire Awesome of Course. Stakes-placed winner Petiteness, by Chief's Crown, gained notoriety as the dam of Grade 1 winner and sire Scorpion. The Group 3-placed winner Adored Slew, by Seattle Slew, became the dam of stakes-placed Silver Traffic. Affirmatively's winning daughter Crazy for You, by Pleasant Tap, is the dam of Australian Group 3 winner Afraah.

The immediate family of Straight Deal has branched throughout the world with continued success. Included in her expansive family tree are the champions Regal Gleam, Caerleon, Bimelech, Black Helen, Bridal Flower, Affectionately, Allez France, Personality, Zoman, Relaxing, and Easy Goer, and Grade/Group 1 winners Royal Glint, Vision, Al Mamoon, La Gueriere, Ordway, Sea Hero, Hero's Honor, Easy Now, Cadillacing, and Tweedside.

Additional Notable Spendthrift Mares

Noblesse Mossborough x Duke's Delight, by His Grace. English champion three-year-old, winner of the 1963 Epsom Oaks and Musidora Stakes.

Rose O' Neill Lord Putnam x Beckygale, by Blenheim II. Winner of the Hollywood Oaks, Interborough, Santa Maria, Distaff, Vagrancy, and Sheepshead Bay Handicaps.

Cantadora Canthare x Madiana, by Pont l'Eveque. Argentine Oaks winner.

La Dauphine Princequillo x Baby League, by Bubbling Over. A granddaughter of blue hen La Troienne.

Affectionately Swaps x Searching. Champion.

Amiga Mahmoud x Miss Dogwood. Winner.

Alamosa Make Tracks x Secreta, by Embrujo. Stakes winner.

Bella Figura Count Fleet x Miss Dogwood

Bernares II Timor x Besarabia, by Cairngorn. Argentine stakes winner.

Boudoir II Mahmoud x Kampala. Irish stakes-placed winner.

Cantadora II Canthare (FR) x Madiana (ARG). Chilean stakes winner.

Call Card Alibhai x Good Call, by Case Ace. Stakes winner.

Camerola Prince Canarina x Campeona, by Filon. Argentine stakes winner.

Chop House Porterhouse x Recess, by Count Fleet. Stakes winner.

Corvette Black Out x Campeona, by Filon. Argentine stakes winner.

Crowned Queen Royal Charger x Pagan Worship, by Hyperion. Clipsetta Stakes winner

Donna Farewell x Blanca, by White Jacket. Argentine One Thousand Guineas winner.

Gallatia Gallant Man x Your Hostess, by Alibhai. Schuylersville Stakes winner.

Gay Hostess *Royal Charger x Your Hostess, by Alibhai

Gerts Image Mr. Music x Bolo Gert, by Bolo. Stakes winner

Gold Digger Nashua x Sequence. Stakes winner.

Metatela Yantorno x Mirra, by Guatan. Argentine Stakes winner.

Miss Dogwood Bulldog x Myrtlewood. Stakes winner.

Miss Fleetwood Count Fleet x Miss Dogwood. Winner.

Ondine II Timor x Owe Nothing, by Owen Tudor. Four-time Argentine stakes winner.

Regal Pink Red God x Welsh Crest, by Abernant. English stakes winner.

Ripa Pride of Kildare x Gold Spi, by Gold Stand. Five-time Australian stakes winner.

Sequence Count Fleet x Miss Dogwood. Winner.

Starlet Nearula x Sansonnet, by Sansovino. English stakes winner.

Success Turn-to x Miss Disco, by Discovery. A half sister to Bold Ruler.

Triple Orbit Gun Shot x Fantine Busher, by Mr. Busher

Amiga Mahmoud x Miss Dogwood, by Bull Dog. Stakes-placed. A great granddaughter of Myrtlewood.

Babuska My Babu x Tsumani, by Cientifico

Beau Jet Jet Pilot x Beaugay, by Stimulus

Belle Epoque Beau Sabreur x Hogmanay, by Umidwar. French stakes winner.

Charged Princequillo x High Voltage, by Ambiorix

Fall Aspen Pretense x Change Water. Stakes winner and 1994 broodmare of the year.

Grecian Queen Heliopolis x Qbania, by

Questionnaire. Coaching Club American Oaks winner

Growing Up Maxim x Macie Margaret, by Sir Greysteel. Stakes winner.

Lady Wayward Dedicate x Spring Tune, by Spy Song. Stakes winner.

Mid Hour Ambiorix x Past Eight, by Eight Thirty. A half sister to Lady Be Good and Time Tested.

Miss Ardan Ardan x Impulsive, by Supremus. Canadian Oaks winner.

Plotter Double Jay x Conniver, by Discovery. Stakes winner.

Red Tulip Jet Pilot x Popularity, by Alibhai. Stakes-winning granddaughter of Busher.

Sequence Count Fleet x Miss Dogwood, by Bull Dog. Stakes-winning granddaughter of Myrtlewood. Dam of Raise a Native's stakes-winning dam, Gold Digger.

Thataway Polynesian x Wayabout, by Fairplay. Stakes winner.

Tulle War Admiral x Judy Rae, by Beau Pere

Chapter Fourteen

COMBS' THOROUGHBRED CLUB OF AMERICA ADDRESS

Leslie Combs II was honored at the Thoroughbred Club of America, and gave the following address at the club's facility at Keeneland Racecourse in 1968.

"Mr. Toastmaster, Mr. President, Ladies and Gentlemen:

To be selected as the honored guest of this, the 37th annual testimonial dinner of the Thoroughbred Club of America is one of the proudest moments of my life. In accepting the pin and scroll symbolic of honorary lifetime membership in the club, I want to thank each of you – my neighbors and friends – from the bottom of my heart. As I look over the names of the past honored guests, I am overwhelmed with a deep feeling of humility mixed with pride; humble when I try to measure my small contribution to the great sport of Thoroughbred racing with theirs, but proud of the opportunity which you have given me to stand beside them. In a nostalgic mood, may I recall briefly some of them who are no longer with us.

The first honored guest was Colonel E. R. Bradley, of Idle Hour and Derby fame. Had he nothing more than give us La Troienne, he would have been renowned. Hal Price Headley and Louie Beard, the patron saints of Keeneland; Mrs. Payne Whitney and Mrs. Dodge Sloane, those two great ladies of the turf; Mr. William Woodward; Joseph E. Widener, Warren Wright, John Hertz, William Jeffords, William DuPont, Jr. – all outstanding breeders and importers of Thoroughbred stock who are directly responsible for many of our outstanding horses of today. Mr. Arthur

Hancock, founder of Claiborne, so ably carried on by his son. Arthur Hancock, Jr., himself an honored guest, and Mr. James Fitzsimmons, affectionately known as "Sunny Jim" and legendary among trainers. These, and many like them, left a priceless heritage and it is well for us to remember.

The history of the Thoroughbred Club of America is symbolic of the growth of Thoroughbred breeding and racing. Founded in 1932 by 15 local horsemen, the club roster has grown to more than 1,000 members from every state in the Union, and in the dominion of Canada. With spacious club rooms and a fine library, the club attracts visitors from all over the world. It has acquired both a national and international status.

So it is with racing and breeding. International racing is a reality today, and with further development of jet air transportation, horses racing on both sides of the Atlantic in a single season will be a frequent occurrence. Shipping from New York to California and Florida – and vice versa – to compete in a single race is already commonplace.

More and more Americans are racing abroad in England, Ireland, and France. The International race at Laurel has been a great stimulant, and we welcome more foreign owners to compete in our great races here.

In breeding, the same is true. The development of air transport has accelerated also the process of internationalization of breeding stock, both here and abroad. Today's pedigrees have become so cosmopolitan that it is virtually impossible to attribute them to being representative of any country in particular.

For many years it was a one way street, but the French, beginning with Relic in 1951, learned that the infusion of American blood was a real shot in the arm to their bloodlines. Even the British, since they abolished the Jersey Act, are finding our blood most useful. One of the leading British writers has gone so far as to say, 'There is little doubt that the really significant improvement in the speed of the Thoroughbred during the last 20 years has been made in the U.S.A. American progress has been built on the twin foundations of persistent buying of the fastest stock, and the strict application of the racecourse test.'

Of course, for the sake of the Stud Book, a horse's nationality is of necessity depending upon the country which it is foaled, but this form of classification can be very misleading. More often than not, an examination of the pedigree will show a mixture of British, French, Italian, and American blood. All this is good and serves to revitalize the bloodlines.

In my own case, we have stallions at Spendthrift from six different countries, but their pedigrees may be said to be international.

I have always been interested in breeding Thoroughbred horses, having come by it honestly from both sides of my family. In 1937, when I decided to venture into the business, it was only natural that I would select the Blue Grass of Kentucky, where I was born and raised, as a base of operation.

I was fortunate to be able to purchase a part of the old Elmendorf Farm of my great-grandfather (Swigert) with money left to me by my grandmother. "Spendthrift," the champion of 1879 bred by my great-grandfather, seemed an appropriate name for the farm. I could only purchase 121 acres of it, but it has grown so that now I have a bear by the tail and can't turn him loose. I started with a one-girl office – and at this point, I want to express to Louise Judy my appreciation for her 25 years of loyal service, and acknowledge how fortunate I am to still have her as my right hand.

During the war years (World War II), there was a highly significant development both to Keeneland and to breeders in this area. Due to wartime restrictions, breeders found it impossible to ship their yearlings to Saratoga for the annual sales that had been the only market for many years. Something had to be done about it, so a group of local horsemen organized the Breeders' Sales Company (now a division of Keeneland) and made an arrangement with Keeneland to use its facilities to hold a sale. The first sale was held in a tent in the paddock and, to the surprise of everyone, was an instant success. It grew by leaps and bounds, opening up a whole new untapped market in the Midwest.

It was only natural that breeding of Thoroughbreds should spread to other states like sprouts off the main tree. The main tree has been Kentucky, which has furnished her sister states a steady flow of bloodstock much as England for so many years supplied us with some of the best Thoroughbreds.

In 1965, 19 states made significant contributions to the total foal registration of 18,000 for that year, and of course you know the foal registrations for the current year will exceed 20,000. According to the Florida Horse, there were only five Thoroughbred farms in Florida in 1947. They say there are now approximately 170 farms, which produced 1,400 registered foals, and any time a Florida horse wins a race, the whole world is informed it was a Florida-bred. This is good promotion.

I am of the opinion that good horses can be bred and raised anywhere good grass will grow, but you have to have good stock to breed from – both stallions and mares. I believe Kentucky is the best place to raise fine horses – and a taste of that good Spendthrift (spring) water will move up any horse. You can't get away from the fact that the figures show that over the last nine-year period, as reported in the *Blood-Horse*, Kentucky produced only 22.6 percent of the registered foals, which accounted for 39.9 percent of the stakes winners in those years.

But Kentucky breeders cannot stand on their laurels of past years. They must continue to upgrade their broodmare bands by constant culling of poor producers and the infusion of new, live blood. We have the greatest concentration of top stallions in the world and we must keep it so.

Sharp competition from other states has served to unite Kentucky breeders for the first time in my memory. There is a greater spirit of cooperation than I have ever known. In this connection, I would like to pay special tribute to the Thoroughbred Breeders of Kentucky for the great work it has done in publicizing the performance of Kentucky-breds, and in giving the breeders the voice of authority. This organization (TCA) has made a highly significant contribution to the success of the Keeneland sales, and deserves the whole-hearted support of every Kentucky breeder.

Nevertheless, much remains to be done in this great industry. The whole thing has grown like "Topsy" in many ways, without rhyme or reason. It is doubtful if there is any other business with so many ramifications that knows so little about itself. As one writer put it:

'Considering the number of dollars invested in the farmland, horses, racetracks, and other assets, the Thoroughbred industry is possibly the biggest business in the United States which has only a vague notion as to where it has been or where it is going.' The plain fact is that racing and breeding as a whole has never studied its own economics.

To remedy this situation, the Thoroughbred Owners and Breeders research, with a wide knowledge of the horse industry, to formulate plans for a nationwide survey in order to provide basic facts upon which the industry, in all its phases, may safely plan for its economic growth and development.

If such a survey is to be of real value, it must have the cooperation of all interests in racing. From state racing commissions and racing associations through owners, breeders, trainers, jockeys, and others whose livelihood depends upon it. I believe this proposal is of vital importance to the industry as a whole, and I urge each one of you to cooperate to the fullest extent to make the survey truly meaningful.

Looking back over my years at Spendthrift, while there have been many changes in both breeding and racing, in the final analysis the formula for success – if there is one – is essentially the same. Breed the best to the best and hope for the best, and remember the first horse past the post is still the winner. The real joy in the game and the true spirit of the sport is love of the horse and the wonderful people who are in it. As has been truly said: 'Take this away and there will be no racing – only races.'

A lot of people ask me how to go about picking out a yearling. The old timers had the following formula:

Eight Points Necessary to Constitute a Good Horse

Two of a deer

Two of a fox

Two of an ox

First: Round body and flat leg

Second: Small ear and bush tail

Third: Full breast and broad hips

Fourth: Full eye and bony cheek – and you have to be lucky.

In closing, I want to take this opportunity to pay tribute to two people without whose encouragement, loyalty, and understanding Spendthrift, as it is today, would have been only a dream – my wife Dorothy, for her love and inspiration, and my Uncle Brownell, who has taught me what I know, and who gave me a start with the great blood of Myrtlewood."

Chapter Fifteen

DOROTHY ENSLOW COMBS

Gracious, charming, and sparkling were all words used to describe the personality of Dorothy Enslow Combs. Her old-world southern charm and genuinely warm personality complimented the affable wit and engaging demeanor of Leslie. Together, they worked as an unbeatable partnership that entertained diplomats, world leaders, millionaires, and movie stars with their annual Kentucky Derby parties and social gatherings held at Spendthrift Farm.

The annual Kentucky Derby party and breakfast before the races on the first Saturday in May was considered one of the premier events of the season. Dressed in tuxedos and gowns, guests would flock to Spendthrift Farm on the night before the Derby to attend the annual festivities where the mint juleps and bourbon flowed. The catered affair was held on the farm's grounds under elegant white tents, complete with music and a dance floor.

"Dad (Leslie) sold a lot of horses at those parties," said Brownell Combs. "Mom (Dorothy) was the perfect hostess, and dad was the perfect salesman. The more people drank the more horses they bought. The revelry went well on into the night."

Following the Derby breakfast, the Combs' and their clients would climb on leased coaches and head for Louisville. The journeys were always festive, and the best way to get invited to ride on a Spendthrift coach was to be a celebrity or spend a lot of money purchasing Spendthrift horses. One of Leslie's favorite selling tools was keeping a stock of "Old Spendthrift" bourbon on hand for the journey, which he had specially bottled for the event.

In 1967, Leslie purchased the first official Spendthrift party coach, and nicknamed it the "Blue Goose." The bus was named after Leslie's grandmother's old blue Packard. Dorothy's father had a private railroad car with the moniker as well.

Among the guests entertained on the Spendthrift coach by Leslie and Dorothy were two future presidents: California Governor Ronald Reagan and Michigan Representative Gerald Ford.

"My mother was the perfect hostess and really loved entertaining," recalled Brownell Combs. "She made everyone feel at home. She came from a prominent family in West Virginia, and was raised with old southern values. She was a gracious lady, with a very big heart. There was always room for one more at the table or in our house. She was also instrumental in supporting my father in all of his endeavors."

Dorothy Louise Enslow was born into social prominence on October 22, 1902, in Huntington, West Virginia, to lawyer Frank Bliss Enslow and his second wife Juliette (Buffington) Baldwin.

The Enslow family arrived in Huntington in 1871, one year prior to the incorporation of the city. Frank was a dynamic figure whose career took him down many diverse paths. He worked as a lawyer, capitalist, banker, and became the one of the organizers of Columbia Gas and Electric Company. As a respected lawyer and counsel, Frank is credited as being one of the founding fathers of Huntington. He became a diversified real estate developer and property owner, and constructed some of the larger buildings in downtown Huntington. He also served as the president of Huntington National Bank, and invested in many commercial and manufacturing ventures.

Frank combined an astute business acumen with a flair for leadership. Although he was considered to be one of the most influential men in the West Virginia Democratic party, Frank never ran for office. He was so highly regarded by his contemporaries that they suggested he run for governor or the senate.

Frank's first wife, Julia Garland, died in 1897 after a lengthy illness. He then married the socially prominent Juliette Buffington, the daughter of Huntington's first mayor, on April 16, 1901.

Dorothy's upbringing as the daughter of one of the most influential families in West Virginia provided her with all the opportunities available to a wealthy young socialite. She was educated in the most genteel southern values, and met the most eligible young men. Her beauty and sincere personality drew a large number of suitors, but none walked away with her heart until Leslie Combs.

After an eight-month sojourn working at his uncle's coffee planting and export business in Guatemala, a restless Leslie landed a job in 1923 working at the American Rolling Mill (Armco) sheet mill in Huntington for 35 cents an hour.

Around this time, Leslie met Dorothy at a social function and charmed her with his quick repartee and engaging humor. After a brief courtship, the young couple married in 1924, and moved in with Enslow's widowed mother. Leslie worked as a teller at the Huntington National Bank until they were able to afford their own home. By the mid-1930s, the family portrait was complete with the addition of Brownell and his sister, Juliette.

In a sad and horrific twist of fate, Dorothy's 63-year-old mother was found beaten and strangled in her bed. The crime, which is considered one of the most heinous in Huntington's history, has never been solved.

In 1937, Leslie and Dorothy moved to Lexington and purchased the first 120.6 acres of Spendthrift Farm. Over the following decades, Spendthrift would grow to more than 5,000 acres, and the name would become synonymous with Thoroughbred breeding world wide.

Although Leslie is credited with aiding the evolution of modern Thoroughbred marketing and syndication, Dorothy was involved in the racing aspect of Thoroughbred ownership.

Gold Digger, the dam of Mr. Prospector, carried Dorothy's orange silks with the blue hoops to victory against the likes of Tosmah and Queen Empress in the 1966 Columbiana Handicap.

In addition to her hostess duties at Spendthrift Farm, Dorothy was well known for her philanthropic involvement. She was the chairman of the Flamingo Ball held annually at Hialeah racetrack in Florida, which was held to benefit the American Cancer Society. The ball was believed to have earned more money from horsemen for the ACS than any other function at the time.

Tragedy once again struck the Combs family when it was discovered that Dorothy was stricken with pancreatic cancer. With dignity and grace, she passed away at her home on Spendthrift Farm on November 20, 1968, at the age of 66.

Friends said that Leslie was never quite the same after the death of his beloved friend and partner. Even the victory of Spendthrift-bred Majestic Prince in the 1969 Kentucky Derby provided little solace to Combs in his grief.

"Dad was never quite the same after my mother died," Brownell said. "He lost a zest for life that my mother fueled in him. It never came back. He missed her terribly. It was a blow to us all."

Upon his death, Leslie Combs willed a majority of his multi-million dollar estate to cancer research in the name of his wife. The Dorothy Enslow Combs Research Facility, located at the Lucille Parker Markey Cancer Center in Lexington, is named in her honor.

Chapter Sixteen

REVIVAL AND REORGANIZATION

Advanced age and the loss of his friend and life partner Dorothy took a toll on Leslie Combs in spite of the vast success that Spendthrift experienced in the late 1960s and early 1970s.

Majestic Prince won the 1969 Kentucky Derby, Leslie reigned as the leading consignor at the Keeneland sales as his yearlings set one world record after another, and Spendthrift-bred Caracolero became the farm's 10th stakes winner for the year after winning the 1974 French Derby. All of it made a limited impact on the aging Leslie who appeared to be losing interest in the farm and its operations.

In March 1968, rumors flew that the original tract of Spendthrift would be subdivided and syndicated for $25 million. Leslie would not entirely substantiate the rumor, but was quoted in *Daily Racing Form* as saying, "I'm preparing to give up much of the original Spendthrift to the subdividers."

The rumor turned out to be a farce or a publicity ploy, and Combs retaliated in a 1969 interview with the *Lexington Herald*.

"Of course there's not a darn thing to it," a feisty Combs told the *Herald*. "In fact, I'm getting tired of issuing denials. If somebody came along with $35,000,000 or $40,000,000 in cash I might listen to him. But nobody has yet, and until then I'm not interested. Although three or four fellows have tried to get me to list the place on the big board (the New York Stock Exchange)."

The wildest rumors of a Spendthrift sale were reported on November 12, 1969, in the *Lexington Herald* when it was disclosed that

Johnny Carson, the popular host of "The Tonight Show," was purchasing the farm in partnership with David Werblin, former owner of the New York Jets, for a reported $20 million. The rumor appeared in the *New York Daily News* column "Suzy Says" written by Suzy Knickerbocker. Werblin, a longtime Spendthrift client, owned the successful racehorse and sire Silent Screen.

Combs told the newspaper that he had "casually mentioned" to Werblin about putting the farm up for sale, but that a price had not been discussed and the matter was not talked about seriously.

Carson's publicity agent, Al Husted, addressed the rumor stating that Carson "doesn't want to comment about it," and explained that the talk show host did not discuss business ventures with the media. Werblin's secretary, Barbara Rudd, further substantiated that Werblin and Carson had no plans to buy a horse farm. She spoke to Carson who had seemed surprised by the news.

The erratic rumors of a pending sale were not the only red flags that signaled discord in the Spendthrift dynasty.

A series of tragic barn fires caused Spendthrift to close to visitors in March 1969 after the third blaze in three weeks and fifth in six months destroyed a barn near the main stallion complex. Five stallions were removed from the complex when the fire was discovered around 5 p.m. on Sunday, March 18, approximately 45 minutes after the gates were closed to visitors. Luckily, no horses were injured. Combs estimated that the damage was in excess of $25,000. Fayette County arson investigators launched an investigation into the matter, and performed lie detector tests to employees on the farm after a similar incident occurred on March 9.

Arson was suspected in the series of barn fires, although the cause was listed as "undetermined." Although the barns were patrolled by hired security guards after the initial fire, anyone could have slipped through the gates as there was no way to monitor the number of guests coming and going. Combs explained to the *Lexington Leader* that all the barns had been checked for outdated wiring, and others had been repaired. He told the newspaper that he couldn't think of any reason why someone would want to burn down the barns.

Twenty broodmares were killed in a barn fire on the Greenwich Road annex of Spendthrift Farm No. 3 on April 16, 1973. The blaze was reported by a farm employee at approximately 3:30 p.m., but by the time firemen arrived the barn was burning out of control. The fire was investigated, but the cause was not immediately determined.

In 1974, 73-year-old Leslie, tired and disgruntled, turned over the farm's operations to his son, Brownell. A skilled horseman and successful businessman, Brownell never followed in the shadow of his illustrious father. He was the owner of Livestock Underwriters, Inc., a successful insurance business in Lexington, and had made his own way in the world with limited assistance from his father. However, when Leslie asked Brownell to run Spendthrift he responded to the call and came home.

"Many people in the business were shocked when this happened," Brownell recalled. "My father and I were not particularly close. The farm, truly, was in a shambles. The barns and facilities were outdated, dad wasn't paying close attention to the business end of things, and it was pretty much a mess. He had really lost interest in the business after my mother died. Everything was starting to fall apart."

Not only had Leslie lost interest in the farm, but he had not paid his taxes. The Internal Revenue Service verified that Leslie had paid no income tax from 1970-1972. In the summer of 1974, the IRS sent him a bill for $166,000 in back taxes owed. Leslie filed suit against the IRS in the fall of 1974 disputing the claim.

According to the May 5, 1975 *Louisville Courier-Journal* report, court records revealed that the IRS did not allow several of the deductions Leslie had claimed on returns. They also questioned his income reporting regarding the sale of certain horses.

In 1971 and 1972, the IRS said that Leslie "understated the taxable income from Subchapter S. Corp. of his wholly owned corporation Belair Farms, Inc., by $102,000. Some $27,000 of this was the 'fair rental value' of the use of a 10-room house as a personal dwelling, and a five-room house for a 'personal servant.'"

Leslie also failed to report the $135,000 in payments from Livestock Underwriters, Inc. as dividends on his 1970-72 tax returns. He was allowed several depreciation deductions following the IRS audit totaling $13,000 on racehorses, and the aging stallion Gallant Man.

"Dad (Leslie) was aware that the business was changing, and he didn't like aspects of that change," said Brownell. "He was losing interest, and failing on the business end. It was time to update operations at Spendthrift, and bring them in step with the established farm traditions."

The task facing Brownell was not an easy one, but he remained undaunted. His background as a horseman and businessman was multifaceted. Brownell grew up surrounded by such horses as Nashua, Idun, Myrtlewood, and Jet Pilot. It seemed natural that he would take out his trainer's license as a teenager. The interest in training horses was diverted by the necessity of an education. After briefly attending Brooks School in North Andover, Massachusetts, Brownell returned to the University of Kentucky where he graduated with a Bachelor of Science degree in Business Administration, and attended graduate studies in Clinical Parasitology. Still unsure of his exact path, Brownell ventured into law at the University of Virginia. Ultimately, an interest in aviation led him to join the Air Force, where he reached the rank of captain. While assigned to the Strategic Air Command, Brownell served as a defense and security services officer. After receiving an honorable discharge, he built and managed the Spendthrift Training Centers located in Kentucky and Florida, and raced a small string of horses.

Brownell became the new general manager of Spendthrift Farm in 1974, and his wife, Linda, an accomplished equestrian, managed the equine operations. His primary objective was keeping Spendthrift's traditions intact while updating the business methodology. Part of Brownell's philosophy included consolidating the farm's assets by selling parcels of acreage and culling the broodmare band.

"The operation had just gotten too large from a management perspective," Brownell said. "It was just too difficult to maintain thousands of acres scattered here and there, and there were too many mares that were not bringing in a profit. There were changes in the labor force; it was hard to find good people to work the entire operation. We sold horses, some land, and realized the need to update the stallion roster. Dad, as chairman of the board, had more than a say in things, but the management of updating operations was left up to me."

The changes occurred swiftly. Brownell syndicated champion three-year-old Wajima for a world-record $7.2 million in the fall of 1975. That December, he received an appointment to the Kentucky State Racing Commission. In 1978, Brownell and Washington lumberman Joe Layman purchased a half-interest in 1977 Triple Crown winner Seattle Slew for $3 million. Seattle Slew retired to Spendthrift Farm at the close of his racing career, and was syndicated for a world-record $12 million. Horse of the Year Affirmed, winner of the 1978 Triple Crown, was owned and campaigned by his breeder and longtime Spendthrift client, Louis Wolfson. The talented son of Exclusive Native retired to Spendthrift, where he was syndicated by Brownell for a new world record of $14.5 million. The son, who had learned from the master, organized 25 syndicates worth $1 million and over.

"We had a great year when Affirmed won the Triple Crown," Brownell reminisced. "Seattle Slew scored a great win over him (Affirmed) in the Marlboro Cup, J.O. Tobin won champion sprinter honors, and Caro led the sire list. We had obvious success, and it was a great year."

Brownell and Linda also came up with a viable solution for the labor problem. They hired new graduates of the Irish National Stud farm management program and employed them at Spendthrift. Many prominent Kentucky Thoroughbred farm owners and managers of Irish origin can trace their humble beginnings to Spendthrift Farm.

"Brownell didn't receive much praise from his father for his accomplishments," recalled former Spendthrift vice president of operations Arnold Kirkpatrick. "They never really got along, and I think Leslie was jealous of Brownell. On one hand you can understand why. He (Leslie) built the farm from the ground up, and here comes the son to take over the operation and make changes. He had a tough time turning over the business, and second-guessed him on occasion. You can see both sides of the equation, although Brownell never got a fair shake from his father, I don't think."

The reformative years of Spendthrift paved the way for what appeared to be a bright new era in the early 1980s. Thoroughbred racing had gone global in a big way. American-bred horses were making a major impact by winning the most prominent races in Europe. As a result, a new group of increasingly wealthy Arab, Asian, and European horsemen came to Lexington to buy horses, and yearling prices soared. Brownell traveled to France and England, where he purchased yearlings at the Deauville (France) and Newmarket (England) sales. The Thoroughbred business was at its zenith, and everyone seemed to profit.

Spendthrift's global expansion included standing the graded stakes winner Don Roberto, by Roberto, at Roland de Chambure's stud in France. Don Roberto became the first son of American-bred English Derby winner Roberto to stand in Europe.

The boom in the Thoroughbred market reeled in a new group of wealthy clientele eager to purchase horses and farms to put them on. As a result, a portion of Spendthrift's legendary fame was put on the market for a tidy sum.

Leslie rejected a proposed sale for part of Spendthrift in December 1982, after a group of investors including his son-in-law David M. Trapp, coal company executive J. L. Jackson, and William Bricker made an offer of $30 million for 40 percent of the large commercial breeding establishment. According to *Daily Racing Form*, Jackson and Bricker were partners with Spendthrift in Equites Associates, a company that purchased a 50 percent interest in the farm's yearling crops for two years prior.

According to Brownell, part of the farm was offered for sale as an estate planning measure. Leslie, as chairman of the board, retained 88 percent of the farm, while Brownell owned the remainder. The deal, considered a limited partnership if it had come to fruition, would have placed the farm's value at approximately $75 million.

Kirkpatrick told the *Form* that if Leslie, who was 81 at the time, passed away it would "create a $50- to $70-million inheritance tax bill." By selling a large portion of the farm, the tax liability of Leslie's heirs would be substantially reduced.

"Those of us dedicated to the continuation of Spendthrift Farm know that a huge inheritance tax bill could bring it to its knees," Kirkpatrick emphasized. "And if this deal falls through, we will just have to try something else."

In January 1983, Leslie made the decision to declare Spendthrift a publicly traded company, and sell shares on the New York Stock Exchange. The transaction divided 5.9 million shares for Brownell and 612,552 shares for Leslie with an average price per share of $5.41. Everyone seemed to want a piece of the pie. By August 1983, 4.2 million shares in Spendthrift were sold for a total of $31.7 million. Approximately one-third of the owner's shares were sold by the end of 1983 for about $35 million.

The farm had found a strategy to offset the tax liability issue, or so it seemed. Spendthrift's chief assets were land and horses. The eager shareholders assumed they could make money as the value of Thoroughbreds spiraled into the millions.

The law of averages states that everything that goes up must come down. And so it was with the yearling market. During the 1985 July yearling sales prices dropped significantly and investors began to question the viability of heavy spending without the possibility of a lucrative return. It was the first hint that a dramatic downturn in the market was imminent, and that the future of Spendthrift was teetering in the danger zone.

CHAPTER SEVENTEEN

THE FINAL YEARS

Spendthrift's decade of prosperity in the mid-1970s and early 1980s provided a brief reflection upon the farm's former glory days, and the management spent money as if the boom would go on forever. Mounting debts, a downturn in the Thoroughbred yearling market, and the public's lack of confidence in the stability of the farm's syndication all contributed to the domino effect which led to the eventual demise of Spendthrift Farm.

"There were a lot of bad business decisions made," Brownell recalled. "We should have never syndicated the farm; it isn't like there was something tangible for the public to grasp. About the time we syndicated, everything went to hell in the Thoroughbred yearling market. I spent so much time traveling and trying to market interest in the farm that I wasn't aware of some of the decisions being made until it was too late. Then I got sick."

Brownell, who became one of the founding members of Breeder's Cup in 1985, journeyed world-wide in order to promote interest in the farm's stock options. After two years of non-stop travel, the stress took its toll. In 1984, Brownell was diagnosed with a heart condition, and his doctor recommended that he adopt a less stressful lifestyle.

"I was never at the farm," he said. "It was very stressful traveling all over the world trying to sell an interest in Spendthrift. As a result, I didn't really know what was going on. Sometimes I would only receive bits and pieces of information, and a lot of it wasn't correct."

One of the first major stallion relocations that signaled a problem at Spendthrift occurred in 1985, when long-time farm client Louis

Wolfson, the breeder and principal owner of 1978 Triple Crown winner Affirmed, made the decision to move the successful stallion to Calumet Farm to stand alongside his old rival Alydar.

"It was a blow when we lost Affirmed," Brownell said. "But looking back, you can't blame him (Wolfson)."

In August 1985, Cincinnati real estate developer Manuel D. Mayerson came forward with an offer of $57 million for controlling interest in Spendthrift stock. According to the *Louisville Courier-Journal*, a letter of intent was signed stating Mayerson's intent to purchase the Combs' 8.9 million shares of Spendthrift stock, at $6.43 per share. The agreement also said that Mayerson would offer to purchase the five million remaining shares owned by 1,500 public shareholders if the sale was completed.

The newspaper reported, without disclosing identities, that several members of the Thoroughbred industry had stated that Spendthrift stock prices had dropped significantly – from its initial $12 per share offering in 1983 to $5.62 per share on the day following the offer and $4.37 a week later. Only a week prior to Mayerson's offer, Leslie had turned down a bid of $3 per share ($27 million) from Richard F. Broadbent, the founder of Bloodstock Research, and Robert Hagopian, then president of the Kentucky Horse Center. In August 1983, 4.2 million shares were sold in Spendthrift Farm through private placement at $7.50 per share, for a total of $31.7 million.

Leslie attempted to refute the decline, and stated that "the decision to sell wasn't an indication that there was a lack of confidence in the company." He commented that no one in the Combs family was interested in taking over the Spendthrift legacy.

"None of them (my grandchildren) give a damn about the property," a disgruntled Leslie told the *Courier-Journal*. "It's such a big thing. It's got to have someone to take care of it."

Mayerson purchased 133,000 shares of the initial stock offering in 1983, and became a partner in several Spendthrift racing syndicates, including Rhoman Rule, who finished last in the 1985 Kentucky Derby.

"I've always wanted to own a horse farm but never dreamed it would be Spendthrift," Mayerson enthusiastically told the *Courier Journal*.

The dream never came to fruition.

The *Lexington Herald-Leader* reported in early September 1985 that Mayerson was unaware that Seattle Slew would be moved after he had made his offer two weeks previously. He still expressed a desire in purchasing a controlling interest in the farm in spite of the 1977 Triple Crown winner's transfer to Three Chimneys Farm near Midway, Kentucky. However, Mayerson would not comment to the newspaper whether the change in circumstances would necessitate a revision in the initial offer.

After the announcement had been made to sell controlling interest in Spendthrift, the Seattle Slew syndicate members elected one of the stallion's original owners, Mickey Taylor, as the new syndicate manager. Taylor, who replaced Brownell, accepted Three Chimney's offer to stand the 1977 Triple Crown winner alongside his newly-retired champion son Slew o' Gold.

"I was tired and I wasn't in good health," Brownell said. "It was unfortunate, but time to step down. I retired as the board chairman in 1985, and dad (Leslie) accepted the post. We were all getting sick of the horse business by this time. The Mayerson deal fell through, and here we were, back at square one."

Spendthrift announced on April 18, 1986, that it would sell all of its broodmares (120) and the entire 1986 foal crop in a farm dispersal at Keeneland's November breeding stock sale. All the yearlings would be consigned to the Keeneland July, Saratoga, and September sales. The announcement also stated that the farm would put 1,200 of the remaining 2,000 acres up for sale, while retaining 800 on the main farm. The decision to sell the horses and land was prompted by a restructured loan arrangement of $16 million which would allow the farm to reorganize as a stallion complex only. The terminology used in the announcement stated that the sale of all horses was prompted by "a major restructuring of operations."

John Post and Keith Nally, then members of Spendthrift's executive board in charge of daily operations, said that the sale of all breeding stock "will provide the company (Spendthrift) with enough cash to pay bank indebtedness and establish a strong liquidity position. Furthermore, this will greatly reduce the farm's overhead and operating expenses without sacrificing net income."

Brownell, who had removed himself largely from the daily operations of the farm at this point, commented to the *Herald-Leader* that the reorganization was a "wise move."

"All the bad press the farm has had the last several months, I can think nothing can be more damaging than that," he assessed. "I feel if the farm can get out of the pages of the newspapers and back to what it's structured to be, it will be much better off."

On December 10, 1986, Leslie announced his retirement as Spendthrift chairman for the second time in six months. The farm's shares plummeted to 87.5 cents per share – the lowest point since the farm went public in November 1983. The company reported a $6 million loss for the first quarter of it's fiscal year, and fell short in sale projections for the November breeding stock sale – desperately in need of an additional $2 million to repay debts.

"I'm too old to be fooling with it," grumbled Combs in a *Herald-Leader* interview on December 10, 1986. "There isn't anybody right now (to recommend as chairman). We'll just have to wait and see how this thing comes out."

The "thing" that Leslie was referring to was negotiating a restructuring of $30 million in bonds issued by Spendthrift as a public company in 1984. Interest payments on the bonds totaled $3.5 million per year, and were supposed to be paid in September and March. The company was unable to make the September payment of $1.7 million in a timely fashion, although it was eventually paid.

The newspaper stated that then-Spendthrift president Hagopian had made an announcement in September stating that the company was in the process of renegotiation through Prudential-Bache, although company spokesmen could not substantiate the statement. Nor had Spendthrift held an annual shareholder's meeting for the year, and none was scheduled. Nally, identified at that time as a company director, told the newspaper that he "thought" a shareholder's meeting might be held in the spring of 1987.

"The chaos continued," Brownell reflected. "We were in too deep. There was no other choice than to file bankruptcy. There were too many bad decisions made, and not enough people on the same page. Mass confusion at the end. The farm was just struggling to survive."

Spendthrift filed for protection from their creditors under Chapter 11 of the bankruptcy code in December 1988, listing their debts at $48.7 million and $7.6 million in assets. The lawsuits from investors soon followed, including fashion designer Calvin Klein who had been one of 14 investors filing suit after they had put up $32 million for a one-third ownership in Spendthrift four months prior to the stock being offered to the public.

A group of investors came forward in 1989 with the intent of restoring the farm to a level of its former glory. Spendthrift client Curtis Green, William du Pont III, Henry "Cap" Hershey, and W. Terry McBrayer purchased the ailing farm for $5.25 million.

"I think they'll do a good job with it," Leslie told the *Herald-Leader*. "They have the money, they have time. They're starting out at the bottom. I'd just like to see Spendthrift go on because I started it."

The new owners, out of respect to the 87-year-old Leslie, asked him to serve as chairman for their new venture.

"I'm too old," he snorted. "I don't want any responsibility. All I want to do is just enjoy things, get up in the morning and do what I want to do. I'm going out for dinner every night this week. I like parties. Is there anything wrong with going to the races with beautiful ladies? Two or three? Safety in numbers..."

On May 19, 1989, all lawsuits were dismissed after a decision was reached by a U.S. District Court jury in San Francisco, California, that Brownell and Garth Guy, an investment banker who had filed the private placement documents, were not at fault.

The trial, begun on March 2, included 14 individual testimonies filed by investors who claimed that Guy's $4.2 million fee had failed to be mentioned in the stock offering, that the value of Spendthrift property and assets had been inflated, and that they had been promised that no losses would be suffered. Investors were seeking reimbursement of their $12 million investment, interest, punitive damages, and treble damages under the federal racketeering act. They also alleged misinformation and lack of disclosure regarding the documents used in the private placement offering. Lawsuits filed against attorney Charles Hembree and his Lexington, Kentucky-based law firm, who aided in arranging the private sales of shares in the farm, had also been dismissed on April 25.

In the midst of the recriminations, lawsuits, and resignations, Leslie maintained an active social life during the final years of his life. He spent his winters at the condominium in Bal Harbor, Florida, and the spring and summers in the mansion at Spendthrift Farm. Leslie frequently attended the sales and Thoroughbred races with a beautiful woman or two attached to his arm. Although he never remarried, he was never without constant female attention.

A charmer to the very end, Leslie enjoyed reminiscing about the horses, syndications, deals, and world-record sales toppers that made him a legendary figure in the Thoroughbred industry. He recognized that the Thoroughbred industry had changed dramatically since his heyday, but that he had been one of the innovators responsible for that change.

In March 1990, an 88-year-old Leslie returned to Kentucky to die. The enigmatic and legendary horseman who built Spendthrift Farm into one of Kentucky's most fabled Thoroughbred nurseries died from pancreatic cancer at 3:30 p.m. on April 6, 1990, at the University of Kentucky's Albert B. Chandler Medical Center. He left his $13 million estate to fund the building of a cancer treatment center at the University of Kentucky named in honor of his wife, Dorothy, and to Centre College.

Leslie received many tributes from friends and associates, but perhaps Hall of Fame trainer Jimmy Jones summarized it best.

"He was a fantastic man," said Jones, who conditioned Kentucky Derby winners Tim Tam and Iron Liege, in an interview with the *Louisville Courier-Journal*. "He probably had more to do than anybody else with the creation of modern stallion syndication and bringing up the price of yearlings to where they were bringing respectable prices. He brought people into the business, and he got the prospective person to Lexington, and once they got here they really got the fever and before you know it, they became owners. He was a pillar of the turf."

Over the following years, Spendthrift Farm changed hands on five occasions. The farm was foreclosed upon in 1993, and put up for absolute auction. The remaining 711 acres, name, perched eagle logo, and royal blue and orange silks were purchased for $7 million by Metropolitan Life Insurance Company. A lawyer and officials for the insurance company said that their intent was to find a buyer who would uphold the farm's longstanding traditions.

The farm was once again put up for a court-ordered bankruptcy auction on May 5, 1994, to settle the final debts. The description of the farm, auctioned off by Swinebroad-Denton, Inc, read as follows: "This legendary farm is to be sold in two tracts. Tract A is 496 acres, and includes the 6,400 square foot main residence. This mansion has six bedrooms, four and a half baths, a beautifully landscaped swimming pool and pool house. Two manager's houses and six tenant houses are part of this tract. This portion has seven barns with a total of 97 stalls, plus the stallion complex, which includes the breeding shed, four stallion barns with 49 stalls, and a utility building with two receiving stalls. All rights to name, colors, and trademark shall be included in the purchase of Tract A. Tract B is 140 acres with one residence. It includes two barns with a total of 31 stalls."

Ted Taylor, a Birmingham, Alabama, attorney purchased the famous farm for $2.56 million, or $5,250 per acre – a startling bargain for a farm of Spendthrift's magnitude.

After several years of ownership, Taylor sold Spendthrift to the partnership of horseman Bruce Kline and the Nastasi and Anderson families for $4.25 million in 2000. In turn, Kline sold it to the current owner, California real estate developer and storage unit mogul B. Wayne Hughes, for an undisclosed sum in 2004. The farm is currently an active breeding operation and stands several stallions.

In spite of all the changes in the Thoroughbred industry, the legacy of historic Spendthrift endures and the name continues to remain synonymous with good Thoroughbreds.

"If you've got the land you've got to have good horses to put on it," Leslie said in an interview. "As sure as the good Spendthrift spring water flows out of the ground, that's what the business is all about...land, horses, people, and bringing it all together. All I ever wanted to do was raise a good horse, like my great grandfather did, and I've come pretty darn close."

Appendix I

SPENDTHRIFT FARM STALLIONS

Affiliate, ch., 1974, Unconscious – Swinging Doll

Affirmed, ch., 1975-2001, Exclusive Native – Won't Tell You. Triple Crown winner, entered stud 1978

Agrarian, bay, 1931, Sickle – Mary Jane, entered stud 1937

Alibhai, ch., 1938, Hyperion – Teresina, entered stud 1941

All Hands, dk. b or br., Turn-to – Best Risk, entered stud 1960

Al Nasr, b., 1978, Lyphard – Caretta, champion older male in France

Alto Ribot, ch., 1964, Ribot – Parlo

Ardan, b., 1941, Pharis – Adagartus, entered stud in France in 1947, French Derby winner, Prix de l'Arc de Triomphe winner

Armageddon, b., 1949-1972, Alsab – Fighting Lady, entered stud 1956

Artic Prince, br., 1948, Prince Chevalier – Artic Sun, entered stud 1952

Arturo A, ch., 1957, Argur – Santa Rosa, entered stud 1964

Assagai, dk. b. or br., 1963-1986, Warfare – Primary II, champion turf horse 1966

Australian Star, b., 1957, Star Kingdom – Rustling, entered stud 1962

Babington, b., 1959, Tatan – Bellezza

Bald Eagle, b., 1955, Nasrullah – Siama, entered stud 1961, champion older horse 1960

Battle Joined, b., 1959, Armageddon – Ethel Walker, entered stud 1963

Beau Pere, b., 1927-1947, Son-in-Law – China, died prior to covering any mares in the U.S.

Begorra, b., 1949, Bimlech – Begum II, entered stud 1958

Bend's Me Mind, Never Bend – Top Round

Bernborough, 1939-1960, Emborough – Bern Maid, entered stud 1949, multiple SW in Australia

Big John Taylor, b., 1974, Speak John – She Figures

Billings, ch., 1945, Mahmoud – Native Gal, entered stud 1940

Black Mountain, b., 1961, Tudor Minstrel – Portage

Blue Times, b., 1941, Olden Times – Cocoblu

Bold Hour, dk. b. or br., 1964, Bold Ruler – Seven Thirty

Bold Irishman, dk. b., 1938, Sir Gallahad III – Erin

Brogan, Nijinsky II – Drumtop

Cabildo, b., 1963, Round Table – Delta

Cap Size, blk., 1961, Sailor – Demree

Captain's Gig, dk. b. or br., Turn-to – Make Sail

Caro (Ire), gr., 1967-1989, Fortino – Chambord, winner of French 2,000 Guineas

Chicuelo, blk., 1938, Ariel – La Chica

Clem, ch., 1954, Shannon II – Impulsive, entered stud 1960

Clem Pac, b., 1961, Clem – Pacifica II

Cojak, b., 1973, Cohoes – Fight On

Comte de Grasse, ch., 1949, Count Fleet – La Libertie, entered stud 1954

Cougar II (Chi), dk. b. or br., 1966-1989, Tale of Two Cities – Cindy Lou, entered stud 1974, champion turf horse 1972

Cornish Prince, br., 1962-1985, Bold Ruler – Teleran

Creme dela Creme, b., 1963-1977, Olympia – Judy Rullah

Crewman, ch., 1960, Sailor – Twelve O' Clock

Crimson Satan, ch., 1959-1982, Spy Song – Papila, champion 2yo colt 1961

Dark Star, br., 1950, Royal Gem II – Isolde, entered stud 1954, KY Derby winner

Dead Ahead, b., 1959-1978, Turn-to – Siama, entered stud 1963

Decidedly, gr., 1959, Determine – Gloire Fille, KY Derby winner

Delta Oil, gr., 1969, Delta Judge – Grey Oil

Dewan Keys, ch., 1975, Dewan – Eleven Keys

Edmundo, Owen Tudor – Weighbridge

Eternal Prince, b., 1982, Majestic Prince – Eternal Queen

Exclusive Native, ch., 1965-1983, Raise a Native – Exclusive, entered stud 1970

Exclusive One, ch., 1979, Exclusive Native – La Jalouse

Fairway Phantom, roan, 1978, What A Pleasure – Imanative

Fleet Nasrullah, dk. b., 1955-1979, Nasrullah – Happy Go Fleet

Foolish Pleasure, b., 1972, What A Pleasure – Fool-Me-Not, KY Derby winner

Futuramatic, b., 1947, Eight Thirty – Heritage, entered stud 1951

Gallant Man (Ire), b., 1954-1988, Migoli – Majideh, entered stud 1959, Belmont Stakes winner

Golden Act, ch., 1976 – 2000, Gummo – Golden Shore

Goal Line Stand, b., 1970, Graustark – Dinner Partner

Good Investment, b., 1965, Nasrullah – Vestment, entered stud 1969

Great Union, b., 1935, Sir Gallahad III – My Flag

Green Hornet, b., 1959, *My Babu – Ellen's Best, entered stud 1967

Grey Legion, gr., 1975, Secretariat – Show Stopper

Guillaume Tell, ch., 1972, Nashua – La Dauphine

Hadagal, b., 1931, Sir Gallahad III – Erne

Hail to All, b., 1962, Hail to Reason – Ellen's Best, Belmont winner

Hechizado (Arg), 1976, Cambremont – Moonrise (Arg)

Hill Rise, b., 1961, Hillary – Red Curtain

Huguenot, ch., 1977, Forli – Captain's Mate

Intrepid Hero, b., 1972-1980, Forli – Bold Princess

Ivermark, ch., 1933, Teddy – Symphorosa

Irish Lancer, b., 1957, Royal Charger – Tige O'Myheart, entered stud 1962

Jacomar, ch., 1937, Jack High – Gay O'Mar

Jaipur, dk. b. or br., 1959, Nasrullah – Rare Perfume, entered stud 1963, Belmont winner, champion 3yo 1962

Jean Pierre, ch., 1964, Prince John – Evilone

Jester, Tom Fool – Golden Apple,

Jet Master, b., 1949, Jet Pilot – Mattie J., entered stud 1955

Jet Pilot, 1944, Blenheim II – Black Wave, entered stud 1948, KY Derby winner

J.O. Tobin, dk. b., 1974, Never Bend – Hill Shade, champion 2yo in England, Eclipse Award-winning co-champion sprinter

Junge Savage, b., 1966, Indian Hemp – Foolspoint

Kentucky Gold, b., 1973, Raise a Native – Gold Digger

Kenty, b., 1933, Teddy – Lady Emmaline,

Kennedy Road, b., 1968, Victoria Park – Nearis,

King Cole, 1939-1952, Pharamond II – Golden Melody

Knave, ch., 1952, Faux Tirage – Trick, entered stud 1959

List, ch., 1968, Herbager – Continue

Life Policy, ch., 1951, Princequillo – Stirred Up, entered stud 1955

Lords, b., 1979, Hoist the Flag – Princessnesian

Lord Avie, b., 1979, Lord Gaylord – Avie, champion 2yo

Magesterial, b., 1977-1994, Northern Dancer – Courting Days

Majestic Prince, ch., 1966-1981, Raise a Native – Gay Hostess, KY Derby and Preakness winner

Mashua's Dancer, b., 1968, Raise a Native – Marshua

Mehmet, ch., 1978-1997, His Majesty – Soaring

Mister Gus, b., 1951-1966, Nasrullah – Fichu, entered stud 1957

Muscovite, b., 1977, Nijinsky II – Alyne Que

*My Babu, b., 1945-1970, Djebel – Perfume II, entered stud 1950, 2000 Guineas winner

My Gallant, ch., 1970, Gallant Man – Prudate

My Request, ch., 1945, Requested – Sugapud, entered stud 1951

Nalur, ch., 1953, Nasrullah – Lurline, entered stud 1958

Nashua, b., 1952-1982, Nasrullah – Segula, entered stud 1956, Belmont winner, Preakness winner

Nasomo, ch., 1956, Nasrullah – Blue Eyed Momo, entered stud 1964

Nasty and Bold, b., 1975-1999, Naskra – College Bold

Native Royalty, b., 1967, Raise A Native – Queen Nasra

Never Bend, dk. b. or br., 1960-1977, Nasrullah – Lalun, champion 2yo 1962, entered stud 1964

Never Give In, ch., 1957, Never Say Die (GB) – Myrtle Charm, entered stud 1962

Norseman, ch., Umidwar – Tara, entered stud 1945

Northern Majesty, b., 1979, His Majesty – Misukaw

Northern Jove, gr., 1968-1994, Northern Dancer – Junonia

One Eyed King, b., 1954, Nasrullah – Siama, entered stud 1961

Orbit Dancer, ch., 1973-1999, Northern – Triple Orbit

Over Arranged, ch., 1969, Staunchness – Eleven Keys

Pilot, ch., 1956, Jet Pilot – War Shaft, entered stud 1964

Pluck, b., 1961, Double Jay – Nut Brown Maid

Premier Ministre, b., 1976, Cannonade – Pixie Tower

Pretense, dk. b. or br., 1963-1987, Endeavor II – Imitation

Princely Native, ch., 1971-1988, Raise A Native – Charlo

Prince John, ch., 1953-1979, Princequillo – Not Afraid, entered stud 1957

Privileged, b., 1934, Sir Gallahad III – Concession

Proctor, ro., 1977, Graustark – Overpowering

Proud Clarion, b., 1964-1981, Hail to Reason – Breath O' Morn, KY Derby winner

Provocative, b., 1946, Roman – Dusk II, entered stud 1953

Rainy Lake, ch., 1959-1980, Royal Charger – Portage

Raise a Native, ch., 1961-1988, Native Dancer – Raise You, entered stud 1964, champion 2yo 1963

Restless Wind, ch., 1956, Windy City II – Lump Sugar

Requested, ch., 1939-1960, Questionaire – Fair Perdita

Royal Charger (Ire), ch., 1941-1961, Nearco – Sun Princess, entered stud 1947

Royal Clove, b., 1954, Royal Charger – Clovelly, entered stud 1961

Seaneen, ch., 1954-1972, Royal Charger – Tir an Oir, entered stud 1962

Seattle Slew, dk. b. br., 1974-2002, Bold Reasoning – My Charmer, entered stud 1962, Triple Crown winner, moved to Three Chimneys 1986

Sebring II (Ire), b., 1959, Aureole – Queen of Speed

Semi Pro, br., 1959, Khaled – Iron Reward, entered stud 1964

Sensitivo (Arg), b., 1957, Sideral – Ternura, entered stud 1964

Sham, b., 1970-1993, Pretense – Sequoia, runner-up to Secretariat in two of the 1973 Triple Crown races

Shannon II (Aus), b., 1941-1955, Midstream (GB) – Idle Words (NZ), entered stud 1949

Silent Cal, b., 1975, Hold Your Peace – False Fashion

Sirlad (Ire), 1974-1982, Bold Lad – Soragna, Italian 2yo, 3yo, and Horse of the Year

Sir Herbert Barker, blk., 1931, Sir Gallahad III – Minima, entered stud 1940

Sir Marlboro, b., 1936, Swift and Sure – Mad Delight

Sizzling John, ch., 1968, Prince John – Tudorka

Soudard, b., 1968, Nord-Sud – Soumida

Supremus, b., 1932, Ultimus – Mandy Hamilton

State Dinner, b., 1975, Buckpasser – Silver Bright

Swaps, ch., 1952-1972, Khaled – Iron Reward, KY Derby winner, champion handicap male and Horse of the Year, stood at Darby Dan for 10 seasons then moved to Spendthrift

Taj Rossi, b., 1970, Matrice – Dark Queen, Australian Horse of the Year

Tenacious, ch., 1954-1967, Challedon – Dorothy B. Jr., entered stud 1963

Time For A Change, ch., 1981-1996, Damascus – Resolver, entered stud 1986

Tipoquill, b., 1952, Princequillo – Hot Slippers, entered stud 1957

Tom Cat, ro., 1960, Tom Fool – Jazz Baby, entered stud 1967

Total Pleasure, ch., 1978, What a Pleasure – Fight On

Triple Bend, dk. b. or br., 1968-1995, Never Bend – Triple Orbit

Tudor Era, b., 1953, Owen Tudor – Erica Fragranes, entered stud 1961

Tudor Minstrel, br., 1944, Owen Tudor – Sansonet, entered stud 1948, champion 2yo 1948, 2000 Guineas winner

Turn-to (Ire), b., 1951-1973, Royal Charger – Source Sucree, entered stud 1955

Turn To Mars, b., 1967, Turn-to – Marshua

Unconscious, ch., 1968, Prince Royal II – Brown Berry

Valdez, ch., 1976-1985, Exclusive Native – Sally Stark

Volcanic, b., 1945, Ambrose Light – Hot Supper, entered stud 1953

Warfare, gr., 1957-1971, Determine – War Whisk, champion 2yo 1959, entered stud 1961

Wajima, b., 1972-2001, Bold Ruler – Iskra, entered stud 1976, champion 3yo male 1975

Wavering Monarch, b., 1979-2004, Majestic Light – Uncommitted

West Coast Scout, b., 1968, Sensitivo – Dandy Princess

Wild Wind, b., 1969, Never Bend – Feisty

Windy City II (GB), ch., 1949-1964, Wyndham – Staunton, entered stud 1953

Yorktown, ch., 1957-1968, Battlefield – Joodles, entered stud 1963

Yukon, b., 1979, Northern Dancer – Gold Digger

Zip Pocket, b., 1964, Nantallah – Barber Shop

STAKES WINNERS

TOP STAKES WINNERS BRED BY LESLIE COMBS

Arewehavingfunyet	Lucky Lucky Lucky
Bint Pasha	Majestic Prince
Deceit	Masked Lady
Landaluce	Mr. Prospector
Francis S.	Myrtle Charm
Gold Digger	Siberian Express
Idun	Silent Beauty
Interco	Smuggly
Lillian Russell	Tumiga

STAKES WINNERS BRED BY LESLIE COMBS & PARTNERS

Combs, John W. Hanes, Mrs. John M. Olin
Betty's Pride, Chalina

Combs, William Floyd (Fairway Farm, Lexington)
Fairway Fable, Fun Forever

Combs, F.J. Heller
Fighting Jodo, Gay Grecque, Incidentally

Combs, Frank J. McMahon
Crowned Prince

Combs, John W. Hanes, Walmac Farm
Clems Alibi, Mr. Hingle, Alexander D.,
Charles Elliott (a horse)

Combs, John W. Hanes
Idun, Irish Lancer, Colfax Maid, Court Affair,
Francis S., Garwol, Do't Alibi, Water Witch, Prince
Eric, Bargain Package, Aqua Vite, Jungle Road,
Francine M., Vaguely Familiar

Combs, Mr. John M. Olin
Prevailing, Shooting Straight, Talent Search, Raise a Bid, Water Blossom, Matchless Native, Gallant Knave, Carezza, Where You Lead

Combs, Mrs. B.W. Martin
Gallina

Combs, Frank Hernan
Dancer's Countess, Mansingh, Clout, Jevalin

Combs, Arthur A. Seeligson, Jr.
Unconcious Doll

Combs, Brownell Combs
Myrtle Charm, Noorsaga, Moon Glory, Carrier X., Hermod, Journalette, Dedimoud, Lady Wayward, Tel O'Sullivan (a horse), Gold Digger (dam of Raise a Native), Tumiga, Masked Lady, Lady Tramp, Alert Princess

Combs, Charles H. Wacker III
Deceit, El Seetu, Guillaume Tell

Spendthrift Farm and Harbor View Farm
Exclusive One, Lover Boy Leslie, My Darling One, Princess Claire

Spendthrift Farm and Wallace Gilroy
Smuggly

Spendthrift Farm, Brownell Combs, Francis Kernan
Northern Aspen

Spendthrift Farm, Equites Associates
Cougarized

Spendthrift Thoroughbred Breeding No. 1
Bint Pasha, Canango

Spendthrift Farm, R. Nervitt, and Four Winds T.B.
Tibullo

Spendthrift Farm and Francis Kernan
Landaluce, Saucy Bobbie, Ecstatic Pride, Bally Knockan, Habitassa, Elle Seule, Wavering Kite

Stakes Winners Bred Under the Spendthrift Farm Name

Active Voice
Adam's Run
Aerostation
Al Mundhir
Angel Island
Arewehavingfunyet
Biricchina
Brorita
Carole's Tale
Charge My Account
Cost Control
Crowned Music
Dancing Gondola
Dancing Partner
Doing It My Way
Double Deceit
Exclusive Love
Fast Forward
Fleet Road
Fleur de Printemps
Goldenita
Great Substance
Holst
Icy Stare
Interco
Intriguing Honor
Lillian Russell
Locust Bayou
Lucky Lucky Lucky
Luigi Tobin
Manicure Kit
Memorable Mitch
Migola
Milord
Muriesk
Muskrat Love
Natania
Northern Jazz
Nymph of the Night
Ohsomellow
Our Reverie
Picturesque
Polite Rebuff
Princess Rapide
Proud Lou
Raise Your Sights
Rascal Rascal
Rossi Gold
Royal Imp
Sanam
Sarba
Sham's Princess
Shamstar
Sharrood
Sheesham
Siberian Express
Smooch
Sugar Charlotte
Truly Met
Village Sass
Zaizoom

Stakes Winners Raced by Leslie Combs
(Not necessarily bred by Combs)

Alert Princess	Lillian Russell
Angel Island	Make Love
Baby Louise	Mashteen
Carmen Dolores	Masked Lady
Crown the Queen	Moon Glory
Crowned Queen	Nashua
Dancing Partner	Never Ask
Doing It My Way	Peninsula Princess
Double Deceit	Rossie Gold
English Silver	Savage Bunny
Exclusive Love	Sea Royalty
Hotsy Totsy	Shady Lou
Huggle Duggle	Shooting Starlet
Irish Cousin	Silent Beauty
Just Jazz	Who's to Know
Lady Tramp	Without Peer
Lady Wayward	Yale Coed

Stakes Winners Raced In Partnership

Combs/Equites Stables
Sugar Charlotte, Princess Rapide, Biricchina, Migola, Lucky Lucky Lucky, Rascal Rascal, Our Reverie, Fleur de Printemps, Northern Jazz

Combs, Curtis Green
Light Crude

Combs, Frank McMahon
Francine M.

Combs, Estate of Helen Gilroy
Mashteen

Mrs. Leslie Combs II
Red Tulip, Gold Digger

Spendthrift Farm, lessee
Fantasy Lover

Stakes Winners Raced Under the Spendthrift Farm Name

Arewehavingfunyet
Argentario
Nymph of the Night

Silent Beauty
Village Sass